Matters of Life & Death

A Catholic Guide to the Moral Questions of Our Time

Gerard M. Verschuuren

Matters of
Life & Death

*A Catholic Guide to the
Moral Questions of Our Time*

 Angelico Press

First published
by Angelico Press 2018
© Gerard M. Verschuuren 2018

For information, address:
Angelico Press
169 Monitor St.
Brooklyn, NY 11222
angelicopress.com

978-1-62138-330-7 (pbk)
978-1-62138-331-4 (cloth)
978-1-62138-332-1 (ebook)

Cover design: Michael Schrauzer

CONTENTS

Preface

We live in a time of very divergent opinions about right and wrong, life and death, sexuality and sex, pro-life and pro-choice, prolonging life and shortening life. We all wonder what can help us to pilot through the raging waters of this turbulent ocean. Where do we find sound judgments in the midst of these debates? What we need more than ever is a moral compass.

Quite a few animals have a built-in compass. We don't exactly know how it works, but it does work. It lets monarch butterflies migrate south in the winter and then back again, it lets honey bees find their nest, and it lets homing pigeons return to their home. But human beings do not have such a compass, so they can go easily off track. They need special artificial tools to help them go in the right direction—tools such as a magnetic compass or a GPS device. But such tools will not help anyone to navigate on moral terrain. That's why we can easily get lost in moral dilemmas, unless we have also some kind of *moral* compass.

This book offers you a Catholic compass. The word Catholic—which comes from the Greek words κατά meaning "about" and ὅλος meaning "whole"—is used in a double sense here. The compass of this book is Catholic in the sense of global and universal—a beacon for all the world to use. It is also a compass that is Catholic in another sense: it has been given to us by the Catholic Church, who has withstood the worst gales of history for more than two millennia. As G. K. Chesterton put it, "We do not really want a religion that is right where we are right. What we want is a religion that is right where we are wrong."

Let me invite you on a quest for what is right and what is wrong under the guidance of a Catholic compass.

1

About Right and Wrong

When it comes to morality and ethics, there does not seem to be much that we can all agree on. The field of morality and ethics is littered with disagreements, disputes, and conflicting arguments. Is there anything we can all agree upon? Isn't there some starting point acceptable to everyone?

Yes, there is. But it may seem meagre at first sight. Probably almost everyone would agree that we have the moral obligation to do what is good and avoid what is evil. It sounds almost trivial. It is almost as trivial as when Socrates said, "It is never right to do wrong." Yet, such general statements give human life a moral dimension and moral foundation and thus enable a civilized life. But disagreement sets in as soon as we try to identify what exactly is good and what is evil, or what is morally right and what is morally wrong.

One word of caution first. The words "right" and "wrong" are also often used outside the realm of morality, when we say that something is wrong in a logical, mathematical, scientific, or political sense. In this book, we will use the words "right" and "wrong" only in the moral sense, equivalent to "good" and "evil." We are *morally* obligated to choose what is good and avoid what is evil—do's and don't's.

So the question is now: What in particular is good, and what in particular is evil? Once we can settle that question, it is probably a small step to agree that we are morally obliged to do what is considered good and avoid what is considered evil. But first we need to fill in the blanks. The fact that all humans—in all times, places, and cultures—agree to some extent that certain acts are morally right or wrong indicates that we are dealing here with objective truths, not subjective feelings. What, then, are these moral truths?

3

How Do We Know What Is Right and Wrong?

In this chapter, we will do some groundwork on which we can build the rest of this book. A first point of dispute is whether morality is something *real*. Moral issues are not settled by experiment; our dispute is grounded in philosophy and metaphysics. Metaphysics has to do with what is real and what is not. Even science cannot exist without some kind of metaphysics. It assumes, for instance, that causality is real, although it cannot scientifically prove so. There is no way we can prove that like causes have like effects, but we presume that they do.

Some philosophers try to confuse us by saying that all we think is real is actually only existing in our minds. Others tell us that even causality is not real, but only a habit of the human mind to associate certain events. We could go on and on, but let us not waste our time on discussions like these. Philosophers are known for putting literally everything into question. They act like criminal lawyers: at trial, they don't have to prove anything in a positive way. All they have to do is raise doubts in the minds of the jurors. There is a joke warning us not to touch anything in a physics lab, not to taste anything in a chemistry lab, not to smell anything in a biology lab, and not to believe anything in a philosophy department.

But perhaps those critical philosophers do have a point. Many people believe that by giving a mighty kick to a stone, they have proved the reality of a stone. Somehow, they do not realize that what comes to our senses is transformed by our brains into a mental model of the external world. Proving reality is not just a matter of kicking or touching a stone—you could also do this in your dream. There must be much more to it, including metaphysics. So kicking is not a very convincing argument. It will certainly not help us determine whether morality is real.

What we usually call "common sense" is a very simple form of metaphysics. Common sense is a basic ability to perceive, understand, and judge things. It is this ability that is shared by ("common to") nearly all people and can reasonably be expected of almost all people without any need for debate. It tells us that there *is* something like an outside world, even when we close our eyes. It tells us also, that there *is* causality in this world, that there *is* order in this world, and that there *are* laws of nature. In other words, common sense tells us that our minds capture the real world the way it is; they do not merely create an illusionary world of fiction, but apprehend things that are there for the "taking," without our having to kick them. We know, for instance, that a bridge designed according to the right laws will stand firm, whereas another bridge collapses because its engineers erred in their calculations or used the wrong laws. Would competent engineers really have better mental habits than their inept colleagues? Common sense tells us that there must be more to it.

In a similar vein, common sense tells us that there are also moral values and moral laws in life. Everyone knows, through common sense, that it is wrong to kill another human being. Ordinary people with "common sense" know right from wrong; that's one of the reasons why they can qualify as jurors in a court system. Even though some do kill other human beings, these people still know, deep down, that it is wrong to do so, but were driven by some passion such as greed, revenge, or anger, which overtook their moral common sense. It might be wise, though, to distinguish "common sense" in morality from "consensus." Consensus is based on common roots and common traditions that not everyone may share, because we come from different cultures. Common sense, on the other hand, is something everyone has in common because it comes with human nature, with being human, regardless of ethnicity and race. When people lose their human nature, we call them inhuman.

When someone denies the existence of the laws of nature, such as the law of gravity, all one can do is invoke the principle of common sense. Common sense tells us there is some kind of *physical* order in nature. Stones that fall today will also fall tomorrow. We cannot prove this today, but we can confidently assume it. Similarly, when someone denies the existence of moral laws and moral values, all one can do is invoke the principle of common sense again. Common sense tells us there is some kind of *moral* order in life: if murder is wrong today, then it will also be wrong tomorrow. This is sometimes called "natural law." Janet E. Smith says about natural law morality that, in a sense, it "is simply plain old common sense.

There are profound and sophisticated ways of explaining natural law, but the practice of reasoning in accord with natural law principals, according to the theory itself, is natural to ordinary people— that is, natural to all mankind for natural law holds that many of the most fundamental precepts of moral reasoning are obvious, that is easily known by all."

Using common sense could also be equated with being "catholic" in its original meaning—that is, being global and universal. Common sense tells us that there is some kind of *moral* order in all of nature, similar to the way there is a physical order in all of nature. Whoever rejects morality is rejecting a vital, undeniable part of human life. Rejecting the reality of morality is as absurd as rejecting the reality of legislation; try to deny legislation, and you will soon get into trouble. The question is, of course, whether moral values and moral laws are there for the taking, or whether we make them up ourselves, as we do in legislation. Although we know, to some degree, how to find out what the laws of nature are—science helps us to do so—moral laws are of a different kind.

What, then, are these moral laws, and are they there for the taking too? Once we acknowledge that morality is something real, we need to settle the question of whether moral actions that we call right or wrong are actually and intrinsically right or wrong. Are they right or wrong by convention or by nature? Where do moral laws and moral values come from? Where do they reside in reality? Let us find out first what does *not* qualify as a basis of morality before we try to dig out its real basis. Unfortunately, there have been many trials to trap morality into something non-moral—possibly as something real but certainly not as moral.

Here is trap number one: Morality comes from past experiences. What is wrong with that claim? Well, killing is morally wrong—but certainly not because we discovered so after we had killed some people or had seen some killings. That would mean we would have to do something wrong before we could know what is wrong. A moral command comes before what it commands, not after. Morality may be corroborated by past experiences, but it is not created by such experiences—in fact, it aims to prevent them. There is mounting evidence that babies as young as six months old make moral judgments and can tell right from wrong. Their sense of fairness begins at a very young age. Researchers have found that, even if an experiment is unfairly rigged so that one child receives more rewards, children will ensure that a reward is fairly split, whereas animals usually fight for the largest piece.

Babies also know the difference between "good guys" and "bad guys"—despite little or no previous exposure to such situations. Based on this natural feeling of right and wrong, they can later be taught more specific rules about "bad guys," such as the "underwear rule": they should not be touched by others on parts of the body usually covered by their underwear, and they should not touch others in those areas. Children sexually abused at a very young age know "intuitively" that they experienced something morally wrong. We learn from this that moral values and moral laws are not discovered through empirical observation, but are somehow "inborn" from early childhood on.

Then there is trap number two: Morality comes from the animal world. Animals do not have morality and cannot have morality. The relationship between predator and prey, for instance, has nothing to do with morality; if predators really had a conscience guided by morality, their lives would be pretty harsh. Animals have social behavior, but not moral behavior regulated by a moral code. As a consequence, animals never do awful things out of meanness or cruelty, for the simple reason that they have no morality and thus no cruelty or meanness. They follow whatever "pops up" in their brains—and no one has the right to morally blame them. When animals seem to do awful things, it is only because we, as human beings, consider their actions "awful" according to our standards of morality. Yet we will never arrange court sessions for grizzly bears that maul hikers, because we know that bears are not morally responsible for their actions. If animals truly had moral rights, their fellow animals, too, would need to respect those "rights."

Then there is trap number three: Morality comes from our genes. What is wrong with that? Why would it be hard to claim that our genes tell us what is morally right or wrong? First of all, those who believe that morality is rooted in their genes must face the possibility that this very belief then is also rooted in their genes—which makes it a belief that comes back like a "boomerang" to hit whoever launched it. Secondly, in the world of genes, there is material substance (DNA), but no truths and untruths that are immaterial—and hence, no intangible moral rights and moral wrongs. DNA is physical "stuff" that can be long or short, light or heavy, but morals cannot be any of these—they have no mass, size, or color. Thirdly, if morality were in the genes, why would we need articulated moral rules to reinforce what "by nature" we would or would not desire to do anyway? Under such circumstances, a moral code would be completely redundant. Instead, the opposite could be argued: morality has the power to overrule what our genes dictate—passions, emotions, and drives. This seems to indicate that morality is at a level "above" the level of genes.

No wonder, then, that far too many people are willing to break a moral rule when they can get away with it. It is hard to believe that they are going against their genes. Everyone knows about moral laws, yet everyone breaks them repeatedly; genes do not seem to prevent this. Unlike the laws of nature, moral laws can be ignored. We have here another flawed attempt at converting moral behavior into a non-moral phenomenon. The rules as to what is morally right and what is wrong do not and cannot come from genes. It is hard to see how non-moral causes such as evolution and DNA could ever produce a moral effect; they are of a completely different nature—as different as the rules of playing chess are different from the pieces on the chess board.

Then there is trap number four: Morality is something acquired —through upbringing, training, disciplining, or education. No doubt, discipline is part of morality. People who are at the mercy of their lusts, drives, and passions may not do the good they ought to do, because they are not disciplined enough to resist their lusts. But that does not mean that morality is merely a matter of being educated, taught, and disciplined. The laws of nature, such as the law of gravity, may have to be taught to us in a physics class or biology class, but they are not only a matter of training and teaching. It is partly through schooling that we know about them, but the laws themselves are not a product of schooling. In a similar way, while parents may help us to understand moral laws and prepare us to do what is morally right, the distinction between right and wrong is not a matter of upbringing. If it were, it would be a product of their own upbringing—which still raises the question of where it began and how.

Then there is trap number five, a very common trap: Morality is a matter of intuition. It may at first be appealing to think that we know "intuitively" what is right or wrong, but the word "intuition" carries a strong subjective overtone—some have it, some do not. This opens the argument up to the attack that morality is not real, but only exists in a person's mind—a thought famously expressed as "many heads, many minds." George Bernard Shaw, for instance, spoke of "different tastes," as if there are many moralities. If morality were merely a matter of intuition or taste, no further discussion would be possible. The best we could say would be that some people have a better taste than others.

Intuition, then, is not a very reliable tool to find out what is morally right or wrong; it comes close to "gut feelings." "Good" is not a matter of what *feels* good. Feelings can never be the standard for judging morality, for we would have to decide next who has the best "gut feelings." It is actually the other way around: morality is the standard for judging feelings. Feelings of revenge, for instance, need to be curbed by morality. Everyone can claim that intuition told him or her what ought to be done, but that in itself does not make such action morally right or wrong; if so, all defendants in court would be entitled to claim that they followed their "gut feelings." Morality determines which moral intuitions are right or wrong.

Then there is trap number six: Morality is a matter of conscience. Like intuition, conscience may seem a good tool in itself to guide our moral behavior. No wonder it is often heralded as the ultimate source of moral good and evil. Ironically, even moral relativists, who deny that morality has any absolute authority, still hold on to at least one moral absolute: "Never disobey your own conscience." They should therefore ask themselves where the absolute authority of a human conscience comes from. How can a person's personal conscience possibly be an infallible guideline for morality? We cannot validly justify that our act was morally right by claiming that our conscience tells us so. Were the Nazis "good" people because they followed their conscience? Both sides in a war conflict believe in conscience and claim that they are right—yet they contradict each other. Both cannot be right at the same time.

To call one's conscience infallible is at odds with the facts: pro-lifers follow their conscience, but so do abortion doctors. Are they both morally right? Only if morality were merely a matter of personal opinions and preferences. However, such a position would lower the standards of morality to our own personal standards, instead of letting moral standards evaluate our personal standards. The idea that one's conscience *creates* moral law is as flawed as the idea that one's consciousness creates the laws of nature. Of course, there is more to a human conscience than this, but let us save that for later.

The Natural Law

If morality does not come from any of the aforementioned sources, and if morality is indeed something real, the question arises: Where do moral laws and moral values come from? Let's call in "common sense" again—in spite of the fact that some say that there is no common morality that we share as humans.

Common sense tells us that there are things that all of us know we ought, or ought not, to do, for the simple reason that we are human beings endowed with morality. There are moral values and moral laws that cannot be ignored, just as there are laws of nature that cannot be ignored. There is a moral order in nature as much as there is a physical order in nature. However, there is a difference between the two orders: laws of nature cannot be violated, yet moral laws can. For instance, you may throw a heavy object upward, but that does not change the fact that the object will eventually fall and might hit you. We can ignore laws of nature, but we cannot go against them. On the other hand, we do have the capacity to violate moral laws—for instance, when we murder another person, we violate the law that all human life is sacred. Yet our action does not make murder morally right, although it allows us to neglect or violate the moral law by acting as if no such law exists. The fact of human *freedom* makes this possible.

Before delving deeper into morality, we would do well to define our terms. We will use the word *ought* in this book more than the word "should," because "ought" is more associated with moral duty and moral correctness than the comparatively neutral "should." Each one of us remembers, from early childhood on, how it feels to be morally obligated, to bump up against an unyielding moral wall. This memory is enshrined in the words "ought," "right," and "wrong."

We will also refer more often to moral *laws* than to moral values, because it is more accepted to speak of "objective moral laws"—similar to "objective laws of nature"—than of "objective moral values." To modern ears, the idea of "objective values" is easily misunderstood as an unintelligible contradiction in terms. Many nowadays tend to associate "values" with the ever-changing value of houses and stock, rather than with ideals which are constant, absolute, and objective. Our secularized age has become crammed with "values"; corporations and universities, for example, are proud to tout their "values." These so-called values allow them to imagine a moral outlook without law, a moral discernment without negative judgments, and moral failure without shame. Politicians often say that certain policies go against their "values," but what they actually mean is that these policies go against their political wishes. As the Boston College philosopher Peter Kreeft astutely remarks, "God did not give Moses 'The Ten Values.'"

Having said this, we pose the question, again, of where our "oughts" and "moral laws" come from. The answer is rather simple; somehow, we "know" what is morally right or wrong. We know what we do not want others to do to us, so we also know what we should not do to others—which is also known as the Golden Rule, "Do to others what you want others to do to yourself" (Tobit 4:15; Matthew 7:12; Luke 6:31). We refer to this rule constantly, especially to judge the actions of others (but not always to judge our own actions!). The Golden Rule is a moral maxim or principle of altruism found in many human cultures and religions, suggesting that it may be a common-sense issue related to a fundamental human nature. Much in the same way that we, without musical training, can judge certain tones to be off pitch, we have moral "perceptions" which tell us that some actions are good and some bad, without having received any explicit training about such kinds of actions. How is this possible? How can every human being know all of this?

Again, the basic answer is "common sense," something that comes with human nature and is shared by all of humanity. St. Thomas Aquinas mentions a general rule: "Good should be done and pursued, and evil avoided." It is a principle that is less definite than the Golden Rule, because it does not specify in detail what is good and what is evil. So where do the details come from? True, there are some important disagreements about what exactly is "good" between different cultures, but beneath all disagreements about lesser moral laws and values, there always lies an agreement about more basic ones.

Peter Kreeft compares this with different languages. Beneath the different words of different languages you find common concepts—this is what makes translation from one language to another possible. In the same way, he concludes, "we find similar morals beneath different mores." There is not a great deal of difference between Christian morality, Jewish morality, Hindu morality, Muslim morality and Buddhist morality, although there is a great difference in the religions themselves. C.S. Lewis tells us that they all have some version of what he calls the "Tao," the natural moral law.

We find this idea in St. Paul's reference to pagans "who never heard of the Law but are led by reason to do what the Law commands" (Rom. 2:14). We find it also in the work of the first Christian philosopher, St. Justin the Martyr, who wrote around the year 150 while living in the turbulent, mostly pagan Roman Empire.

> Every race knows that such things as adultery, and fornication, and homicide are sinful. For example, though they all fornicate, they do not escape from the knowledge that they are acting unrighteously—with the exception of those possessed by an unclean spirit, those debased by wicked customs and sinful institutions, and those who have quenched their natural ideas. For we observe that such persons refuse to endure the same things they inflict on others. They also reproach each other for the evil acts that they commit.

It is mostly through St. Thomas Aquinas that this concept of moral communality has become known as the *natural law*. Its key idea is that moral laws are based on human nature, on the way we *are*. As a consequence, morality is a function of human nature, so that reason can discover valid moral principles by looking at the nature of humanity and society. What we ought to *do* is related to what we *are*. "Thou shalt not kill," for instance, is based on the real value of human life and the need to preserve it. "Thou shalt not commit adultery" is based on the real value of marriage, family, and mutual self-giving love, and on children's need for trust and stability. We share these moral convictions, to some degree, with all of humanity. Every culture in history has had some version of the Ten Commandments.

Natural law rests upon the claim that things have natures and essences that we can detect and that our actions can correspond to. All things possess a nature or essence; they flourish when they act and are treated in accord with that nature or essence—and they wither when they are not. There are many reasons for making this claim. One is the fact that all things act in a predictable fashion; when we learn the properties of oil and water, for example, we can predict certain things about their behavior. Natural law holds that we live in a universe of things that have a nature to them, and that we shall get the best out of these things if we act in accord with the nature that is written into them. When we act rationally, we act in accord with our own nature and reality and with the nature and reality of other things. This holds also for morality. Moral laws and values have a certain foundation in reality—they are based on relationships between human beings and things. Where, for instance, does the moral value of loving one's parents come from? The answer is that the physical and mental constitution of human beings happens to be such that children ought to love their parents in order for them to prosper as human beings. Were our human constitution differently structured, we most likely would have different morals.

This idea is taught, not only by the Catholic Church, but by all the world's major religions and nearly all pre-modern philosophies. It is the idea that the laws of morality, like the laws of physiology, are not rules that we invent but principles that we discover. They are based on human nature, and human nature is essentially unchanging; therefore the laws of morality are also essentially unchanging, just like the laws of physiology. Just as our physiological nature makes it necessary for us to eat certain foods and to breathe oxygen for our bodies to be healthy, so our moral nature makes certain moral rules and values necessary for our souls to be healthy. As G.K. Chesterton observed, you cannot free things "from the laws of their own nature. You may, if you like, free a tiger from his bars; but do not free him from his stripes."

Be aware, though, the natural law is a philosophical concept rather than a scientific one, which means that there is no empirical or experimental evidence to cite. We can prove by sense evidence that something is black or cold or ten feet long; but how can we prove that something is right or wrong, good or bad? The natural law is grounded in the metaphysics of human nature, including the language of the body. So morality must be grounded in part on facts about human biology, which connects the moral order to the physical order of nature. One's morality is always dependent on one's anthropology, and therefore on one's metaphysics. As a consequence, you can't know what is good for man until you know what man is; and metaphysics always comes in, because what man is depends on what *is*. The natural law derives the essential principles of morality from unchanging human nature and its real, objective needs rather than from the changing subjective feelings and desires of individuals.

Thomas Aquinas argues that *reason* should be our guide to morality. The word "natural" in natural law alludes both to human nature, in terms of which the content of morality gets defined, and to the fact that some moral knowledge is accessible to us naturally (as opposed to supernaturally)—through pure reason, that is (as opposed to divine revelation). The precepts of natural law are principles of human activity. Most philosophers agree that we do not need revelation to figure out that some acts are wrong—acts such as murder, adultery, rape, and theft. Our reason is capable of discovering that things have essences, natures, dispositions, and purposes, and that it is good to act in accord with those essences, natures, dispositions, and purposes. Because we can discover this without divine revelation, all of humanity has access to this truth. You don't have to be Catholic for this, although the idea itself is catholic!

The *Catechism of the Catholic Church* explains, "This law is called 'natural,' not in reference to the nature of irrational beings, but because reason which decrees it properly belongs to human nature" (CCC 1955). This text stresses that the natural law is not a law of biology, for it does not apply to "irrational beings" such as animals. But we do need a certain understanding of what human nature is— an understanding that is more than a biological understanding. David Hart rightly remarks that "we cannot talk intelligibly about natural law if we have not all first agreed upon what nature is and accepted in advance that there really is a necessary bond between what is and what should be."

One word of caution, however. Critics of the natural law theory have accused Aquinas of committing a fallacy, which is an incorrect logical argument. The so-called "is-ought fallacy" was identified by the philosopher David Hume, and is sometimes called "Hume's Guillotine." Hume says that we cannot derive how things *ought* to be from the way things *are*. A conclusion that applies to morality cannot be deduced from propositions in which moral terms are missing. Survival of the fittest, for instance, may be the way it *is* in nature, but we cannot infer from this that it *ought* to be that way in human society. In other words, prescriptive statements cannot be derived from purely descriptive ones. It is not quite clear, though, how valid Hume's "principle" is. Some have even jokingly said that, because we cannot derive an "ought" from an "is," we "ought" not to try.

Others have tried to get around this fallacy by defining moral terms in purely natural terms. But this leads to another fallacy, the so-called "naturalistic fallacy," which is the erroneous idea that what is natural (found in nature) can be defined as good in moral terms. In its simplest form, it says "X is found in nature; therefore X is natural; therefore X is good." It creates another fallacy that equates a property such as "good" to a property such as "natural." We cannot argue from the premise "Taking revenge is natural" to the conclusion "Taking revenge is good." Being natural does not automatically make something good; seeking pleasure for pleasure's sake, for example, is not necessarily something that is morally good. When philosophers try to define "good" in terms of natural properties such as "pleasant" or "desirable," they are committing the naturalistic fallacy. A natural concept cannot capture the essential property of a moral concept. A moral concept cannot be redefined in non-moral terms. When we define moral notions in non-moral terms, we betray their moral aspect.

In response to attacks like these on Aquinas, the late Notre Dame University philosopher Ralph McInerny explains that "ought" is already bound up in "is," in so far as the very natures of things have inclinations, dispositions, ends, or goals within them. A clock, for example, is a device designed and used to keep time, so because it "is" a clock, it "ought" to keep the time. If you want to build a bridge that can withstand wind and traffic, you "ought" to follow the laws of nature. In like manner, if one cannot determine good human action from bad, then one does not really know what the human person *is* by nature. For Aquinas, the way a thing "is" also includes its inclinations, dispositions, goals, and ends. He has a richer ontology than most modern philosophers.

Another reason why Aquinas does not commit the naturalistic fallacy is that, immediately after his formulation of the first principle of natural law—"Good should be done and pursued, and evil avoided"—Aquinas points to man's natural inclinations: man naturally inclines to self-preservation, to procreation, to sociability, and to truth about God. So we can only comply with the first principle of natural law by consulting our natural inclinations. Since we *do* have a natural tendency to act certain ways, we *ought* to act certain ways. It is precisely the first principle that prevents Aquinas from falling into naturalistic traps. It is like a principle of practical reasoning in morality, similar to the way theoretical reasoning requires the principle of non-contradiction. Therefore, moral norms are not derived directly from nature, but from the moral command expressed in the first principle. In other words, nature itself is not the foundation of morals, but only plays a secondary role where it informs us about our natural inclinations. Aquinas does not argue from "is" to "ought," but consistently argues from "ought" to "ought," while "is" only plays an intermediary role.

Others have argued that in fact there is some deep connection between "ought" and "is," because nature cannot be seen as something independent of God—it is God's nature. So if nature includes an inherent purpose or function, then that intrinsic purpose bridges the so-called is-ought gap. After all, if humans have a purpose grounded in their very nature as human beings, then they ought to fulfill that purpose. Pope Benedict XVI recently confirmed that "the ought does flow from the is." He meant that once we get a sense of who God *is* and what a human being *is*—created in God's image and likeness—certain "oughts" do flow from what "is." Beneath the "ought" lies the "is"—the natural order, which comes also with inclinations, dispositions, goals, and ends. So we are not dealing here with a simplistic version of the is-ought fallacy.

Because of his concept of natural law, Thomas Aquinas considers moral laws and principles as *self-evident* (known through themselves). It is in that sense that the US Declaration of Independence can state, "We hold these truths to be self-evident." When people claim that they have certain unalienable rights, there is no evidence to support such a claim. When someone asks us why killing another human being is morally wrong, there is nothing we can point to as evidence—it is self-evident. This does not mean, though, that moral laws are data-less "intuitions"; they are knowable only by insight (*intellectus*) into data of human nature, human experience, human understanding, and the order of Creation. Through these rational "intuitions" imbedded in human nature, we discover eternal and absolute moral principles. However, Aquinas adds to this that "self-evidence" is relative, for what is not obvious to some will be objectively self-evident to those who subjectively have more ample experience and a better understanding of other aspects of the matter. So we should expect our moral understanding to grow. This implies that the self-evidence Aquinas claims may not be fully present yet in each one of us.

This explains the fact that there is also something like moral blindness, equivalent to color blindness. Although a blind person cannot see the trees outside, the trees are still there; the existence of the trees does not depend on whether the blind person perceives them or not. In a similar way, a morally blind person may not see the moral laws and values in the universe, yet they are there; their existence does not depend on whether a person with moral blindness can perceive them. Moral blindness can be caused by upbringing, culture, personality, and lust, which may temporarily obscure the self-evidence of moral values, principles, and laws.

Not only are moral laws self-evident, they are also *unconditional*. Most rules we are familiar with are conditional upon a certain goal: if you want Y, do X; if you do not want to attain that goal, the rule is useless. Not so with moral rules and laws. They are unconditional: do X, for you *ought* to do X—no matter what, whether you like it or not, whether you feel it or not, whether others enforce it or not. Therefore, when it comes to morality, we cannot pick whatever we want. We cannot vote to decide whether we condone certain actions —such as slavery and abortion—or not.

President Abraham Lincoln put it well when he challenged the Nebraska bill of 1820 that would let residents vote to decide if slavery would be legal in their state: "God did not place good and evil before man, telling him to make his choice." There is no "prochoice" in morality. Morality obliges us to go, unconditionally, for what is good and right. No more ifs; no more questions asked.

In addition to being self-evident and unconditional, moral laws are also *objective*: they are a "given," independent of us and of any human authority. In other words, they are not invented but have to be discovered. In the words of the *Catechism*, "Objective norms of morality express the rational order of good and evil" (CCC 1751). As a consequence, they are real, not purely mental or a product of the mind. "Objective" means that something is real and true, regardless of whether or not we know it to be true. Something similar holds for laws of nature such as the law of gravity. This law has always been true, even before Isaac Newton discovered the law—it was a discovery, not an invention. Surely, gravity is not a subjective experience, but an objective reality.

If we were to create or invent new moral laws and new moral values, then they would no longer be moral laws or values, and they would no longer be anchored in reality. They would be arbitrarily invented rules of the game—what is "right" in chess is not "right" in checkers. Hence, we would not feel obligated by them, nor guilty when we transgressed them. As C. S. Lewis once put it, "The human mind has no more power of inventing a new value than of imagining a new primary color." We cannot creatively make hate good, or love evil. When we say justice "is" good, we are asserting something about reality, about what really *is*. The fact that people may disagree about specific moral laws does not make morality subjective. Disagreement about objective matters does not prove subjectivity; for if that were the case, every scientific disagreement would become a subjective issue.

In addition to being self-evident, unconditional and objective, moral laws are also *universal*: they are the same for everyone everywhere. They are universally applicable to all of humanity, regardless of race, ethnicity, nationality, culture, or political affiliation. Consequently, morality is a common property that belongs to all human beings. By its very nature, morality is not connected with interest groups or with majority votes. The *Catechism* confirms this: "The natural law, present in the heart of each man and established by reason, is universal in its precepts and its authority extends to all men" (CCC 1956). Although the natural law is not universally obeyed, or even universally admitted, it is still universally binding and authoritative.

No wonder Thomas Aquinas made a clear distinction between the universal "natural law" and the local (legal, civil, or positive) laws made and upheld by local governments. Interestingly enough, without the universality of the natural law, there would not have been any justification for the Nuremberg trials that took place after World War II—or for any other international court, for that matter. From a purely legal point of view, it would not have been right, or even possible, to bring to trial and punish the Nazi perpetrators who had applied the civil laws that were created and implemented by a regime that had come to power through legal channels—for they were "law-abiding" citizens following the law of the land. But from the perspective of natural law, their "lawful" actions were in fact atrocities committed against humanity.

Those denying the universality of moral laws are relativists who privatize and politicize moral laws as if they were merely local civil laws. These moral relativists consider moral laws man-made, private, subjective, and a matter of mere feeling—at best a matter of consensus or a majority vote. They fail to differentiate between moral laws and local laws. According to moral relativism, each one of us is right when it comes to moral matters; according to moral absolutism, on the other hand, some of us may be wrong. Chesterton put it correctly: "Morality is always dreadfully complicated to a man who has lost all his principles." Principles mean moral absolutes—unchanging rocks beneath the changing waves of feelings and practices. Moral relativism, on the other hand, is a philosophy that denies such moral absolutes. This makes Peter Kreeft, in line with Aquinas, exclaim, "In fact, the moral language that everyone uses every day—language that praises, blames, counsels, or commands—would be strictly meaningless if relativism were true."

In addition to being self-evident, unconditional, objective and universal, moral laws are also *timeless*, and therefore unchangeable. The *Catechism* (1958) says: "The natural law is immutable and permanent throughout the variations of history; it subsists under the flux of ideas and customs and supports their progress." Moral relativists would object to this idea, saying that moral values vs. evaluations clearly have been subject to change during the course of human history. However, there is a mix-up here between moral *values* and moral *evaluations*. Moral evaluations are our personal feelings or discernments regarding moral values and laws. Moral relativists think that, in making moral evaluations, we create moral values in accordance with these evaluations. Therefore, when evaluations change, the moral values and laws are said to change as well.

In response to this position of moral relativists, it should be emphasized that evaluations are merely a reflection of the way we discern absolute moral laws and values at a specific time. Whereas moral evaluations may be volatile and fluctuating, moral values and laws are timeless and unchangeable. That is the reason why we can argue about our moral evaluations, assuming some are true and others false. Think of the following comparison: Our current understanding of physical or biological laws constantly needs revision each time science reaches a better understanding of those laws in the way they really are. In the meantime, though, we assume that there are timeless laws of nature, although we may not yet have fully captured them in our current understanding and in our existing evaluations. Something similar could be said about moral laws. Morality is not a function of the clock.

We could illustrate this point a little further. A few centuries ago, slavery was not evaluated as morally wrong, but nowadays it is seen as wrong by most people. Did our moral values change? Our evaluations certainly did, but that does not mean that our moral values did too. Only some people in the past—St. Cyprian, St. Gregory of Nyssa, St. John Chrysostom (c. 347–407), St. Patrick, St. Anselm (c. 1033–1109), and St. Vincent de Paul, to name a few—were able to discern the objective, intrinsic, and universal value of personal freedom and human rights (versus slavery), whereas many of their contemporaries were blind to this value. That is the reason why Martin Luther King Jr. called any unjust (legal) law "a code that is out of harmony with the moral law."

In addition to being self-evident, unconditional, objective, universal and timeless, moral laws are also *absolute*—which means that they are without exceptions. A morality of mere convention, of man-made and thus man-revisable rules of the social game, is not morality at all, only mores. Killing a human being is always morally wrong; stealing is always morally wrong; lying is always morally wrong—no matter who you are and where you are, regardless of your status in society, and regardless of any particular circumstances. Does this mean that there are never situations when killing or lying can be morally right?

Indeed, there might be such situations—especially so when ethical dilemmas arise and choices have to be made. Perhaps killing is not murder when war is necessary for peace. Perhaps stealing is not theft when one is taking a weapon away from a terrorist. Some may counter that this reeks of relativism. But it is flawed to argue that if morality is determined by situations, and situations are relative, then morality must be relative. As Peter Kreeft puts it, "Morality is not determined by situations, but conditioned by it. It determines it partly, not wholly." The fact that the same moral principles must be applied differently to different situations presupposes the absolute validity of those principles.

In other words, killing is always wrong, even in a just war; stealing is always wrong, even when unarming a killer. Yet there may be situations wherein killing or stealing is permissible. Situations may vary, but the moral principles do not. If the standard were as flexible as the situation, then it is no standard at all. Yardsticks have to be rigid. A "situation" may make a deed permissible. Killing for self-defense makes killing not murder; therefore killing for self-defense is morally permissible, although it remains morally wrong. In the words of the *Catechism* (2263): "The act of self-defense can have a double effect: the preservation of one's own life; and the killing of the aggressor. . . . The one is intended, the other is not." It may not be murder, but it remains killing.

Although man's nature and essence are timeless and do not change, accidental situations do. The *Catechism* (1957) acknowledges this fact: "application of the natural law varies greatly; it can demand reflection that takes account of various conditions of life according to places, times, and circumstances." For instance, capital punishment may be morally necessary in a primitive society, but needlessly barbaric in a society with secure laws and prisons; and the moral restrictions on warfare today, with its weapons of mass destruction, must be far stricter than those in the past. "Whenever an exception is made to a moral law, there is always a more general moral law that justifies the exception," says Peter Kreeft. The moral law forbids murder, not necessarily killing. The *Catechism* (1754) says, "Circumstances of themselves cannot change the moral quality of acts themselves; they can make neither good nor right an action that is in itself evil."

Summarized, there are some strong resemblances between scientific laws (laws of nature) and moral laws (the natural law). Both are universal (applicable to everyone everywhere), absolute (without exceptions), timeless (even if we do not know the underlying law yet), and objective (a given, independent of us and of any human authority). They are objective, universal, timeless, and absolute standards, whether we talk about laws of nature in terms of true and false, or about moral laws in terms of right and wrong. Just as "truths are true," even when we do not know they are true, so "rights are right," even though we may not realize that they are morally right. The foundation for the latter claim comes from natural law. In the words of the *Catechism* (1959): "The natural law, the Creator's very good work, provides the solid foundation on which man can build the structure of moral rules to guide his choices."

Is all of the above convincing to everyone? It depends. Even the best arguments will not work for those who are unwilling to listen to them. Such people often do not like what the world looks like with morality in the picture. But they cannot remove morality from the picture. As the *Catechism* (1958) puts it, "Even when it is rejected in its very principles, [the natural law] cannot be destroyed or removed from the heart of man. It always rises again in the life of individuals and societies." To those who say to us, "Don't impose your moral values and laws on me, for you have no right to tell me what to do," we might respond with, "Sure I do."

Rights and Duties

Closely related to matters of right and wrong are the moral concepts of rights and duties. Rights are something other human beings morally owe us and *ought* to do to us; duties are something we morally owe other human beings and *ought* to do to them.

Moral duties and rights go hand in hand and have a natural reciprocity. The duty of self-preservation comes with the right of self-preservation; the duty to seek the truth matches the right to seek it; the duty to work for justice comes with the right to pursue it; the duty to protect life goes with the right of life to protection; the right of receiving religious freedom corresponds to the duty to grant religious freedom; the duty to acknowledge human dignity implies also the right to claim it; the right to live means also the duty to live.

In other words, if "no duties" then "no rights," and if "no rights" then "no duties." There is no duty to own slaves, so there is no right to own slaves; no one has the duty to marry, so no one has the right to be married; no one has the duty to have children, so no one has the right to have children; no one has the duty to die, so no one has the right to die. Once we uncouple rights from duties, fake new "rights" can pop up like mushrooms, invented and claimed on the spot while the question of duty is utterly lost. Such "rights" become *entitlements*, enforced by a legal system—the laws of the land. Entitlements are at best something the government owes us; they are not something we owe the government.

We said earlier that morality may be understood without any special revelation from God, for anyone can discover moral laws and values through the way we *are* and through the way the world *is*. There are many different religions, but there are not many different moralities. However, a morality rooted in human nature would lose its basis if human nature were merely a biological or evolutionary product. To find a solid foundation, human nature has to be anchored in its Creator, God. We do not need to know this in order to know that we have moral obligations; people may very well act morally without knowing *why* they act morally. Similarly, when being active in science, we do not have to know that God created the Universe—although it is hard to explain how science would be possible if the order of the Universe did not come from a Creator who implemented that order. Just as the natural order finds a solid basis in God, so does the moral order.

The concepts of human rights and human duties are based on one of the most important sentences in the *Catechism* (1700): "The dignity of the human person is rooted in his creation in the image and likeness of God." The real basis for natural morality is this super-natural fact. If there really is a Maker of Heaven and Earth, an Author of nature, then his intentions can hardly fail to be relevant to a proper understanding of our moral obligations. The *Catechism*, again (1954):

> Man participates in the wisdom and goodness of the Creator who gives him mastery over his acts and the ability to govern himself with a view to the true and the good. The natural law expresses the original moral sense which enables man to discern by reason the good and the evil, the truth and the lie.

If morality does ultimately come from God, then there can be no morality without God. Do my genes, or any other natural factors, have the right to demand absolute obedience from me? Does society have the right to demand my absolute obedience? Does any person, including myself, have the right to demand my absolute obedience? None of these do! The only authority that can obligate me is someone infinitely superior to me; no one else has the right to demand my absolute obedience. As Fr. Mark A. Pilon puts it, "Western nations today have lost any valid understanding of natural rights because it has undercut the rational grounds for these rights. Rational grounds ultimately require a lawmaker, far above the limitations of human positive law." This means that there are no rights and no duties without God. An absolute law can only come from and be enforced by an absolute Will. The writer Fyodor Dostoyevsky had it right when he said that without God, all things are permissible. Without God, even an oath becomes meaningless.

Interestingly enough, even an atheist such as the French philosopher Jean-Paul Sartre realized that there can be no absolute and objective standards of right and wrong if there is no eternal Heaven that would make moral laws and values objective and universal. As an atheist, he had to conclude that it is "extremely embarrassing that God does not exist, for there disappears with him all possibility of finding values in an intelligible heaven. There can no longer be any good *a priori*, since there is no infinite and perfect consciousness to think it." Because Sartre denied the existence of God (until just before his death), he realized very clearly that he also had to give up on morality by being an atheist. If there is no God and no eternal goodness, there cannot be evil either. As Thomas Aquinas famously said, "Good can exist without evil, whereas evil cannot exist without good."

The German philosopher Friedrich Nietzsche was another atheist to realize how devastating the decline of religion is to the morality of society, when he wrote, "God is dead; but as the human race is constituted, there will perhaps be caves for millenniums yet, in which people will show his shadow." Nietzsche is saying here that humanism and other "moral" ideologies shelter themselves in caves and venerate shadows of the God they once believed in; they are holding on to something they cannot provide themselves, mere shadows of the past. They are "idols" constructed to preserve the essence of morality without the substance.

Nietzsche clearly understood that "the death of God," as he called it, means the destruction of all meaning and value in life. He saw clearly that neither our dignity nor our morality would be able to survive in a world without divine and eternal laws. Jürgen Habermas, a non-religious philosopher, expressed his conviction that the ideas of freedom and social co-existence are based on the Jewish notion of justice and the Christian ethics of love: "Up to this very day there is no alternative to it." This does not mean, of course, that we must believe in God in order to live a moral life. As Nietzsche put it, we can still venerate "idols from the past."

Because of all of this, we must recognize that morality comes from "Above." Moral laws, moral values, moral rights, and moral duties ultimately reside in Heaven. They are real because they come with Creation. We ought to do what we ought to do—for Heaven's sake! The *United States Declaration of Independence* declared that we are endowed by our Creator with certain unalienable rights. When, in 1948, the United Nations (UN) affirmed in its *Universal Declaration of Human Rights* that "all human beings are born free and equal in dignity and rights," it must have assumed the same—that such rights are not man-made, but God-given—but the drafters famously left the term "right" vague in order to achieve passage. The Catholic philosopher Jacques Maritain said, paradoxically, "We agree on these rights, on condition that no one asks us why." The only reason we have human rights is that God endows us with rights.

Therefore, "equality in dignity and rights" would be sitting on quicksand, subject to the mercy of law makers and majority votes, if it had no firm foundation. It is through the voice of God in the natural law that we know about right and wrong, about human rights and human duties. Without God, who is the author of human rights, we would have no right to claim any rights. If there were no God, we could not defend any of those rights we think we have the right to defend. We would have (legal) *entitlements*, which the government provides, but no (moral) *rights*, which only God can provide. John F. Kennedy put it well in his Inaugural Address: "The rights of man come not from the generosity of the state, but from the hand of God." In response to those who say that we should act in a way that is moral "even if God does not exist," Pope Benedict XVI argued that we should do the opposite, living a moral life "as if God existed." Without God, there could be no absolute or objective standards of right and wrong. If these did not come from God, people could take them away at any time—which they certainly have tried to do numerous times.

We have an important distinction here: *rights* are God-given, while *entitlements* are man-made. Some people think of human rights as if they were entitlements that the government gives us. Indeed, we gain entitlements as we age—in the USA, we can drive a car at sixteen, vote at eighteen, and buy alcohol at twenty-one. But we cannot apply this kind of reasoning to human rights. We have rights because all human beings are God's creatures subjected to his natural law; entitlements we only have because we belong to a certain society. Rights are God-given, so that we cannot invent them on our own, while entitlements are something that individual societies invent and promulgate all the time. The government can hand out entitlements, but it cannot give rights away, although it may sometimes try to take them away.

Unlike entitlements, moral rights and duties are universal, absolute, timeless, objective, and nonnegotiable standards of human behavior. The *Catechism* (1978) puts it this way: "The natural law is a participation in God's wisdom and goodness by man formed in the image of his Creator. It expresses the dignity of the human person and forms the basis of his fundamental rights and duties." Therefore, when it comes to morality, we cannot just pick whatever we want. Morality obliges us to go, unconditionally, for what is good and right. Earlier we said that there is no morality without moral absolutes. Now we should add that there can be no moral absolutes without God.

The natural law is one of the most precious gifts Religion has to offer the State. Societies and governments that violate the natural law with their legal laws do not last long. Pope John Paul II envisioned this clearly: "The root of modern totalitarianism is to be found in the denial of the transcendent dignity of the human person who, as the visible image of the invisible God, is thereby by his very nature the subject of rights which no one may violate—no individual, group, class, nation, or State." If moral values were indeed relative, one could never claim, as almost everyone does, that certain human rights are universally applicable to all cultures and all peoples.

What Is a Human Conscience?

For some enigmatic reason, the authority of a person's conscience still ranks high in the polls. Conscience is now the highest court of appeal—it has been given ultimate "primacy," coming close to infallibility. Even moral relativists, who deny that morality has any absolute authority, still hold on to at least one moral absolute: "Never disobey your own conscience." Almost all people have something about conscience that they respect, even if their theory is that conscience is nothing. One wonders how conscience can be so popular. The main reason probably is that the slogan "Follow your conscience" has come to be code for pursuing one's personal preferences and desires.

What is wrong with such a slogan? There is a lot of confusion and ambiguity behind the idea of "just following your conscience." Our conscience has often been compared with technical devices we are all familiar with: a compass, a global positioning system (GPS), a barometer, an alarm, a gas gauge in a car—the list goes on and on. What these analogies get right is that our conscience is indeed a monitoring device—it monitors what is good or bad, right or wrong. What they mask is the fact that the devices referred to are merely tools that may not work properly or may even fail entirely— and so may our conscience.

A real compass, for instance, functions as a pointer to the magnetic north, because the magnetized needle aligns itself with the lines of the Earth's magnetic field—that is, with something outside itself. But it should not be used in proximity to ferrous metal objects or electromagnetic fields, as these can affect its accuracy. At sea, for example, a ship's compass must be corrected for errors, called deviation, caused by iron and steel in the ship's structure and equipment. The compass itself may have a defect. The gas gauge in your car may no longer go down because it is broken, yet the tank may be almost empty. Your GPS system may not work when something obstructs the connection with the satellite high above your head.

In other words, a person's conscience may indeed function like a compass or GPS, but these "monitoring" tools must themselves be monitored and aligned to an outside source, and the same is true of our conscience. Just as a compass needs to be aligned with the Earth's magnetic field and protected from surrounding interference, and a GPS system needs to be "aligned" to the right feed from satellites high in the sky, so a human conscience needs constant alignment. But keep in mind that the fact that our moral compass may sometimes fail does not mean that there is no right direction at all. As in math, we may get our sums wrong, but it does not follow that there is no right answer at all. The question, then, is: What is the "right math" in morality? What is the right feed for our conscience? How do we properly align it, and to what? In short, how do we calibrate our conscience?

The Catholic Church would say that human beings are created with a moral compass pointing, not to the magnetic North, but to the "Above"—to a place where justice reigns and moral laws reside. Therefore, our conscience is not a private "compass" that determines its own North Pole; it has to be aligned to the one and only real "North Pole Above"—otherwise we can easily go off track. The political philosopher Hannah Arendt observed that "just as the law in civilized countries assumes that the voice of conscience tells everybody 'Thou shalt not kill,' [...] so the law of Hitler's land demanded that the voice of conscience tell everybody: 'Thou shalt kill.'" Such things happen when our moral compass becomes a private compass that determines its own direction.

Obviously, there is more to morality than having a conscience and following it. When people say, "Never disobey your own conscience," they forget that one can do things "in good conscience," but also "with a bad conscience." Therefore, a conscience on its own can be good as well as bad. Many people are unaware that they have a moral compass, or have a moral compass that is broken. They are left to follow their genitals in sexual affairs, their curiosity in biomedical research, or their personal desires in matters of life and death, no further questions asked. However, personal desires cannot possibly be the source of morality, because it should be the other way around: Morality judges our desires.

As a consequence, someone's conscience cannot have absolute authority in and of itself. A person's conscience does not speak on its own, but reflects the natural law bestowed on us by God. Our conscience does not create moral laws and values, but merely receives them. This is why we cannot take our conscience as an entirely private issue that we can form at our own discretion. To use another analogy, a compass does not create its own magnetic field. Therefore, a person's conscience is not the highest moral authority there is; it is subject to the supreme authority of the natural law, which comes directly from God.

As Vatican II puts it, "in the depths of his conscience, man detects a law which he does not impose upon himself, but which holds him to obedience." The *Catechism* (1776) calls our conscience "man's most secret core and his sanctuary. There he is alone with God whose voice echoes in his depths." Therefore, when people follow their conscience, it is important they listen to God's voice, not their own. As stated earlier, personal moral evaluations do not necessarily reflect universal moral values. In the words of emeritus Amherst College professor Hadley Arkes, "Conscience is not directed inward to oneself and one's feelings, but outward to the natural law and moral truths."

How can our conscience possibly steer us the wrong way? Because our conscience is dependent upon human reason, it is subject to all of the weaknesses to which human reason is prone, being damaged by Sin since the Fall. This tendency to error means that we cannot treat our conscience as an infallible guide to moral truth. Conscience, like any intellectual ability, can err because the human mind can be more or less mature, experienced, trained, healthy, sophisticated, imaginative, prudent, integrated with passion, etc. As a result of original sin, there is a permanent need for the correct formation or calibration of conscience. Archbishop Anthony Fisher of Sydney, Australia puts it this way: "Conscience is only right conscience when it accurately mediates and applies that natural law which participates in the divine law; it is erroneous when it does not."

We mentioned earlier that there exists something like moral blindness, comparable to color blindness. It is hard, if not impossible, to deny that moral blindness does exist when one considers all the moral evil in the world. One could even question whether every human being has morality. There seems to be some evidence that certain people are *a*-moral—never showing empathy, morality, guilt, or remorse. It is hard to tell whether this behavior is a choice or a disorder beyond one's control. There are certainly people who act in an *im*-moral way by choice. Then there are those who choose to be *anti*-moral as a form of protest, just as there are anarchists and nihilists.

It is always possible to disqualify such choices by calling them disorders, but it is equally possible to reject such explanations. The outcome ultimately depends on our concept of morality. If morality is considered extrinsic to being human, then a person can be a-moral. But if it is intrinsic to being human, there is no way for people to be amoral unless they *choose* to be amoral. It is, says Blaise Pascal, the will that "dissuades the mind from considering those aspects it doesn't like to see." Apparently, much can go wrong with a human conscience, but we are almost always dealing with decisions, moral or immoral. St. Augustine astutely remarks about his stealing pears from an orchard as a child, "I had no wish to enjoy what I tried to get by theft; all my enjoyment was in the theft itself and in the sin." This is an example of the perverse will that chooses evil for its own sake—a consequence of Original Sin in which the will rebels against reason as a slave at the command of passions. Just as the good can be loved for its own sake as something intrinsically desired, so evil can be willed for its own sake. This is when the moral sense becomes desensitized, making evil appear to be good.

Because, as the *Catechism* (1960) says, "The precepts of natural law are not perceived by everyone clearly and immediately," we may need "visionaries" to show us the disconnect that exists between what is right and what we think is right. It is not always right to obey our culture's values; "visionaries" have a transcultural view by which they can criticize the moral laws and values of an entire culture. Just as science needs geniuses like Newton and Einstein to discover scientific laws no one else has seen before them, so morality needs "geniuses" such as prophets and saints to uncover moral laws to which others are blind.

As Jesus would say, "You have heard that it was said [...], But I say to you. . . ." What he actually tells us is that, whether we "see" it or not, he is outlining the way this world was designed by the Creator. Yet some do not "see" certain moral values the way they are, or see them but violate them knowingly. This should not give us any reason to lower our moral standards, as relativists would like us to do. Just as we should not lower standards in school teaching when some cannot make the mark, so we should not adjust moral standards to what everyone can handle or accept. Archbishop Anthony Fisher would say, "If in our sinful world God's law seems unrealistic, the trouble is not with God's law but with the world!"

The fact that we can be morally blind—blinded by upbringing, culture, character, personality, or temperament—explains why we need help to correct a faulty conscience. Therefore, our conscience should be in a perpetual "dialogue with God." A "dialogue" with the self only amounts to a monologue which isolates and alienates us from God, our moral Lawgiver. The one who is supposed to follow the law has no right to make himself the law-giver by becoming a sovereign individual in the place of God and his Church—this would be a form of idolatry. The only authority that can obligate us is someone infinitely superior to us; no one else has the right to demand our absolute obedience. Archbishop Fisher again: "A Catholic must be prepared to accept moral instruction from the Church and never appeal to conscience to make an exception for himself."

Our conscience is like an alarm that alerts us before we sin; when it goes off, we must not ignore it. When a red warning light in our car lights up, we have the problem fixed—not by disconnecting the light, but by fixing what causes it to light up. It is the same with our conscience: we must not silence it. However, when the alarm does *not* go off, this does not mean that there is an "all clear" sign, for we may have intentionally lowered its "volume" or ignored its upkeep. That is how we can willfully manipulate or even damage our conscience. It requires "maintenance service" and needs to be "calibrated" again, often with help from the Church.

Pope Pius XI, in his 1931 Encyclical, said: "We have said recently that we are happy and proud to fight the good fight for the liberty of consciences, not . . . for liberty of conscience." In other words, men have the right to follow their consciences without external interference. The conscience itself is another issue; it is not free to ignore objective truth in making moral judgments. We cannot change freedom *of* conscience into freedom *from* conscience. Let us see now how our conscience should deal with several moral issues that we commonly encounter in our modern culture and society, beginning with human sexuality.

2

Human Sexuality

Sexuality has always been a vital part of humanity; as G. K. Chesterton put it, "There is nothing in any other social relations in any way parallel to the mutual attraction of the sexes." But since Sigmund Freud, human sexuality has become an all-inclusive, all-absorbing part of human life, promoted with slogans like "It's all about sex." Sex may be everywhere, but it certainly is not all there is to existence. We need to place sex back where it belongs, as one of many aspects or dimensions of human life.

A Short History

It is evident that our views on sexuality have changed dramatically during the course of history. However, the Christian view found its origin in Jewish understandings of human sexuality. It is probably best summarized in Ecclesiastes (9:9): "Enjoy the life with the woman you love." Sexuality is seen as a source of joy and pleasure; the *Catechism* (2362) puts it this way, "The Creator himself . . . established that in the [generative] function, spouses should experience pleasure and enjoyment of body and spirit." But there is more to sex than enjoyment; sexuality finds its expression in a marital or nuptial relationship, analogous to the relationship between God and his people. The *Catechism* (2363) is very specific:

> The spouses' union achieves the twofold end of marriage: the good of the spouses themselves and the transmission of life. These two meanings or values of marriage cannot be separated without altering the couple's spiritual life and compromising the goods of marriage and the future of the family. The conjugal love of man and woman thus stands under the twofold obligation of fidelity and fecundity.

Jesus did not come to change the Law, but to perfect the Law. Jesus reinforced the bond between man and woman in marriage, declaring it irrevocable in Mk 10:6–9: "But at the beginning of creation God 'made them male and female.' For this reason a man will leave his father and mother and be united to his wife, and the two will become one flesh. So they are no longer two, but one flesh. Therefore what God has joined together, let no one separate." In addition to marriage, Jesus recommended celibacy as a special service to the Kingdom of God. He did so because celibacy also expresses love, but without a marriage.

Saint Paul described the love relationship between man and woman as a symbol of the relationship between Jesus and his Church. He also repeated Jesus's message about celibacy in his First Letter to the Corinthians (7:1–3):

> Now for the matters you wrote about: "It is good for a man not to have sexual relations with a woman." But since sexual immorality is occurring, each man should have sexual relations with his own wife, and each woman with her own husband. The husband should fulfill his marital duty to his wife, and likewise the wife to her husband.

When the Church grew as an institution and came into contact with the Greek world, it reinforced the idea, found in writers such as Plato and Aristotle, that the celibate unmarried state was preferable to and holier than the married state. At the same time, mainstream Christianity had become infected with a distrust towards bodily existence and sexuality under the influence of Manicheism and similar movements. Manicheists were hostile to the flesh and to sexual activity. They condemned the human body in its masculinity and femininity. Later on, the movement of Catharism proclaimed similar ideas, declaring marriage and procreation evil.

The Church had to deal with the danger of such views. Taking the lead of St. Augustine, who had once been under the influence of Manicheism, the medieval Christian developed the *sacramental* understanding of matrimony by including marriage in the select seven to which the term "sacrament" was applied. A sacrament is often defined as "a visible sign of an invisible reality." The first official declaration of marriage as a sacrament was made at the 1184 Council of Verona as part of a condemnation of Catharism. Marriage was now seen as a sanctification of the Christian couple. The bride and groom confer the sacrament on one another; the Church's representative, usually a priest or a deacon, is simply a witness to the sacrament.

Soon—especially after the Council of Trent in 1563—most writers of moral handbooks in the Catholic Church were canon lawyers who treated marriage in terms of a mutual agreement or a legal contract, with less emphasis on its sacramental character. When the founder of the Society of St. Vincent de Paul, Blessed Frederic Ozanam, decided to marry his future wife, a priest who had hoped for a religious vocation told Pope Gregory XVI that Ozanam had fallen into the "trap of marriage." The Pope quipped, "I always thought we had seven sacraments. Not six sacraments and a trap!"

Gradually, the Church began to confirm more explicitly that marriage, love, procreation, and sexuality are strongly interconnected. More recently, Pius XII tried to strike a balance when he said, "spouses should experience pleasure and enjoyment of body and spirit. Therefore, the spouses do nothing evil in seeking this pleasure and enjoyment. They accept what the Creator has intended for them" (as quoted in CCC 2362). Soon after, Vatican II made sure that all elements of marriage and sexuality were kept in the picture. The *Catechism* (2332) words it this way: "Sexuality affects all aspects of the human person in the unity of his body and soul. It especially concerns affectivity, the capacity to love and to procreate, and in a more general way the aptitude for forming bonds of communion with others." And elsewhere (2337), "Sexuality, in which man's belonging to the bodily and biological world is expressed, becomes personal and truly human when it is integrated into the relationship of one person to another, in the complete and lifelong mutual gift of a man and a woman."

In his Apostolic Exhortation *The Joy of Love* (*Amoris Laetitia* 131–32), Pope Francis adds to this,

> Marriage is a means of expressing that we have truly left the security of the home in which we grew up in order to build other

strong ties and to take on a new responsibility for another person. [...] To opt for marriage in this way expresses a genuine and firm decision to join paths, come what may. [...] Unwillingness to make such a commitment is selfish, calculating and petty. It fails to recognize the rights of another person and to present him or her to society as someone worthy of unconditional love. If two persons are truly in love, they naturally show this to others. [...] This "yes" tells them that they can always trust one another, and that they will never be abandoned when difficulties arise or new attractions or selfish interests present themselves.

Very recently, however, we saw a dramatic twist in the debate about marriage and sexuality. The so-called "sexual revolution" unleashed in the 1960s, aimed to "liberate" human sexuality from the straightjacket of "traditional" morality, specifically the perceived "restrictive" morality of marriage in Christianity. The groundwork had been laid in the 1940s by Alfred Kinsey, who did what he called "scientific research" on human sexuality, published in his so-called "Kinsey Reports." But lo and behold, the "disinterested, impartial observers" of his team were encouraged by Kinsey to sexually experiment with each other, himself, his wife, and invited guests. Some have speculated that Kinsey was driven by his own sexual lusts; some have actually called him a pervert. Yet many praised his "insights"; he inspired, among many others, the founder of *Playboy* magazine. Although he died in 1956, we are still living with the consequences of his actions.

Since then, many have come to see sexuality as completely liberated from the bonds of marriage, monogamy, love, and fidelity. This development has created bad interference for a moral compass.

Body and Soul

At the heart of the Christian message about marriage and sexuality is the Catholic understanding of the relationship between body and soul—or their close equivalents, body and spirit, body and mind, or flesh and spirit. The core idea is that there is more to the body than genitals, and more to the mind than sex. This view is in stark contrast to that which the modern world is promoting—a view that sees human beings as glorified animals, differing from beasts only in degree, their reason being only a more efficient instrument for finding opportunities to feed and copulate. This strongly contradicts the way the Catholic Church sees humans—as beings made in the image and likeness of God, endowed with rationality and morality, consisting of body and soul.

Catholic sexual morality is deeply rooted in natural law. As theologian Janet E. Smith puts it:

> Natural law sexual morality begins with the observation that man has a natural inclination to sexual intercourse, and natural inclinations to loving unions and to having children, and that all of these activities are interrelated. The more we know about the nature of sexuality, of the desire/need of human beings for loving unions, of the desire/need of human beings for having children and to the needs of children, the better we will be able to determine what kinds of actions help us achieve the goods that we seek.

This line of thought can be traced back to St. Thomas Aquinas. He considers marriage a primary human good that has a dual goal: not only the procreation and bringing up of children in a manner suited to their good, but also a "fidelity" [*fides*] that includes exclusivity, permanence, and commitment to being united with one's spouse in soul and body. Consequently, as Notre Dame philosopher John Finnis explains, the kind of wrongful sexual choice most often considered by Aquinas is that of engaging in intercourse with one's spouse without *fidelity*, because one either is thinking of one's spouse in the way one would think of a prostitute, or would be willing to have sex with somebody else if some other attractive person were available. Such depersonalized sex acts Aquinas considers instances of willing against the good of marriage [*contra bonum matrimonii*]. This understanding is key to the sexual morality of Aquinas and the Catholic Church.

Although the word "fidelity" may carry some legalistic and moralistic overtones, fidelity gives marriage its durability. Marriage is not merely a legal contract but a covenant; this is precisely what a man and a woman seek when they make their wedding vows, and fidelity is an essential part of it. Perhaps "love" is a more popular term to use, although it has its own passionate overtones. So the "good of marriage" is twofold: love as well as procreation. It is important to stress that the purpose of marriage is not *only* procreation, for animals also procreate when they copulate, while love is missing in this act. Love is more than sex. Alice von Hildebrand likes to say that in a marriage love is first, not procreation, for if procreation were first, a couple would need a medical certificate of fertility before taking on a marriage; or if they became infertile (for instance, after menopause), they should never have intercourse anymore. Instead, love is first, and from this love arises the ardent desire of fruitfulness as a consequence.

Another important insight of Aquinas's philosophy is the strong bond between body and soul, body and spirit, or body and mind—whichever terminology one prefers. To Aquinas, the soul is the substantial *form* of a human being. Form and matter make up a substantial unity; one cannot have form without matter, nor matter without some form. Applied to the relationship between body and soul, this would indicate that the "form" of the soul gives a specific existence to the "matter" of the body. Body and soul, or spirit and flesh, are two sides of the same coin; the soul is the form of the body, or put differently, the spirit is the form of the flesh. Aquinas embraces the total reality of the human person as an organic composite of spirit and matter, without emphasizing one element to the detriment of the other. This perspective clearly impacts the way the Church looks at sexuality, from two different sides: the bodily part of intercourse and procreation, and the spiritual part of love and fidelity.

In Aquinas's view, body and soul are not individual substances, as they are in Cartesian dualism, which sees the soul as jailed in the prison of the body, waiting to be released. Rather, body and soul are a unity whose nature is comprised of both material substance and immaterial form, so that the body becomes what it is due to the soul. As a consequence, we cannot separate the body from the person, as is done in biology, nor can we treat the soul as separate from the person, as is done in some esoteric philosophies. In the words of Robert P. George, "The idea that human beings are non-bodily persons inhabiting non-personal bodies never quite goes away." What is lost in this approach is the truth that body and soul are a unity, with the soul expressing itself through the body—or in terms of sexuality, love expressing itself through intercourse. There is no such thing as a disembodied soul or a soul-less human body. The body and the soul make for a "psycho-somatic" unity.

Therefore, the soul is not like a pilot in the "ship" of a body, as Descartes saw it. In the Cartesian view, a pilot can be without a ship, and a ship can be without a pilot, so that damage to the ship does not directly damage the pilot. But in the Aquinian view, there is no body without a soul. When the body hurts, the soul hurts, and when the soul hurts, the body hurts. Consequently, when the soul loves, the body loves. The soul loves through the body.

Since there is such a tight connection between the two, there is a spiritual dimension to every bodily act, and every spiritual aspect has a bodily correlate. Key to the body is the spirit, and key to the spirit is the body. One cannot be understood without the other. When it comes to sexuality, a human person is not just a body with genitals, but a body with a soul. Neither is a human being merely a soul, but also a body that can enjoy the pleasures of intercourse and sexuality. The *Catechism* (2332) words this as follows:

> Sexuality affects all aspects of the human person in the unity of his body and soul. It especially concerns affectivity, the capacity to love and to procreate, and in a more general way the aptitude for forming bonds of communion with others.

Aquinas's philosophy has permeated Church doctrine for centuries. But Thomas Aquinas lived and taught in a culture which might be described as objective, deductive, and principle-based. The modern world, on the other hand, has become increasingly subjective, inductive, and experience-based. This calls, perhaps, for a different expression of Church teaching regarding sexuality. Arguably the best overview of how the Catholic Church sees marriage and sexuality in more modern terms can be found in a series of General Audiences in which Pope John Paul II laid the groundwork for his *Theology of the Body*. John Paul II was a Thomas Aquinas for our time, who tried to recast the "jewels" of the faith into a mode and garb which makes them understandable to our age.

John Paul II based his lectures mainly on the first chapters of the

Book of Genesis, offering us an integrated vision of the human person truly worthy of modern man. When God had created the animals, Adam gazed at each of them—at their bodies, that is. He distinguished himself from them as different, because their bodies were different from his own body. He therefore had a consciousness of his own body as revealing his own interior life, his own personhood. As the Pope writes, Adam "discovers the meaning of his own corporality." He comes to realize, in the now famous phrase of John Paul, that his body expresses his person. As the Pope remarks: "The body, in fact, and it alone, is capable of making visible what is invisible: the spiritual and the divine." The human body, then, is more than the sum of its biological parts. Through the biological functions of the body, human personhood is revealed.

When Adam discovered that he was different from all the animals and could not find his "match" among them, he had to come to grips with the age-old question "Who am I?" He could not find an answer to this existential question until he met Eve. By seeing her, Adam knew who he himself was. And by seeing him, Eve knew who she was. In this exchange, they identified themselves. They both discovered that they were a gift from God to each other. It was in this loving relationship that they found their fulfilment—a discovery of their own invisible souls through their visible bodies.

When God created Man and Woman, Adam and Eve, he created them in his own image and likeness. This belief has vital consequences. One consequence is that, since God loves, all human beings are called to love in the same way that God loves. Love is the reason why God created Adam and Eve. Just as God's love was creative, so could their love be creative. In loving each other, they formed a communion of persons, the first nuclear family. When Adam and Eve saw each other, they realized that there are "two complementary ways of being conscious of the meaning of the body." In a word, they discover masculinity and femininity. Adam and Eve entered into a marriage, a union of two persons expressed in and through their different, complementary bodies. It was the first marriage. The free choice to commit themselves to each other was done on the basis of their mutual complementarity, i.e., on the basis of masculinity and femininity.

Adam and Eve realized that their bodies were made for a union between them. But this union was not just of the body. Pope John Paul II calls this experience of unity "the nuptial meaning of the body." This awareness of the nuptial meaning of the body is the fundamental truth about human beings: It is the truth that we are created in and for love. The body is not an object of pleasure or a machine for manipulation but a means of expressing and receiving love. Pope Francis says in *The Joy of Love* (153), "In our own day, sexuality risks being poisoned by the mentality of 'use and discard.' The body of the other is often viewed as an object to be used as long as it offers satisfaction, and rejected once it is no longer appealing." Pivotal is that love in a marriage is a reflection of God's love for us.

What has happened? Sin occurred—a crucial event that changed the face of the earth. John Paul II calls the Fall a "constitutive break within the human person, almost a rupture of man's original spiritual and somatic unity." After the Fall, lust caused Man and Woman to see one another as purely sexual beings. After the Sin, instead of giving, each felt a desire to take the other person, as one does with objects. This desire was manifested in their bodies, and both realized their desire to take advantage of each other.

So they hid their own bodies "to remove from man's sight what is the visible sign of femininity, and from the woman's sight what is the visible sign of masculinity." After the Sin, there clearly is a fundamental change in the body/spirit unity of the human person. From then on, Adam and Eve were each ashamed in the presence of the other, because they knew that they should not reduce the other to an object, and yet, after sin, their desire to take each other was apparent in their naked state.

Lust had entered paradise—the lust to take and seize. "Lust is disordered desire for or inordinate enjoyment of sexual pleasure," says the *Catechism* (2351). This does not mean that the human body is evil, as it is in Manicheism or Catharism. Lust is what Genesis condemns; it is not the body but the person, body-and-soul, that takes and grabs. The Manichean interpretation, on the other hand, held that it was not only lust which was condemned, but the object of lust, the human body in its masculinity and femininity. It changed the object of the lustful look into evil, not the lustful look itself.

This is like declaring the gun, not the terrorist, evil; or the alcohol instead of the alcoholic. The human body is not evil; lust comes from the person. Thus, sexual immorality is sin against one's own body.

For most people, freedom means an absence of any constraints— the right to do as one pleases at any particular time. In this view, freedom means the right to follow any impulses of any kind, including those of the flesh, which is lust. By giving in to the flesh, by living according to the flesh, we allow our freedom to be "taken over" by our passions and emotions. We are no longer free in the sense that we control our passions and emotions—instead, they control us. Freedom is never freedom *from* the truth, but always and only freedom *in* the truth. True freedom does not exist without self-mastery; freedom requires that we be free of any interior compulsion. Self-mastery enables us to free ourselves from any compulsion arising out of our passions and emotions. The *Catechism* (2395) calls this *chastity*: "Chastity means the integration of sexuality within the person. It includes an apprenticeship in self-mastery."

It is obvious that Pope John Paul II, in his *Theology of the Body*, stays in line with Aquinas's conception of body-and-soul when he says, "As an incarnate spirit, that is, a soul which expresses itself in a body and a body informed by an immortal spirit, man is called to love in his unified totality. Love includes the human body, and the body is made a sharer in spiritual love." If the human body could not participate in this characteristic of love, husbands and wives would rather use than love one another.

Like Adam and Eve, husband and wife have a unique relationship to each other. The late Fr. Richard M. Hogan, Associate Director of Priests for Life, puts it this way:

> God allows married couples a unique participation in the power of creation. The animals reproduce, but their offspring are not persons. [...] Only human persons can bring new embodied images of God into our world. Only human beings can give life to new unique persons of equal value to themselves. Each child is another expression of God in this world and will live for all eternity.

In the same way that love in a marriage is a reflection of God's love for us, so is sexuality in a marriage a reflection of God's creative power—the creation of new life. Love and sexuality are part and parcel of a marriage; they call for "fruitfulness" (fecundity, fertility, procreation, or reproduction).

Sexuality without Procreation

But what are we to make of married couples who decide *not* to be "fruitful" and *not* to give life to new unique persons? We are not talking here about the pain of infertility—that we will do in chapter 4. We are talking here about a form of sexuality that explicitly and intentionally excludes procreation from sexuality.

Why is procreation or reproduction such an important part of human sexuality? The natural law answers this question as follows, in the words of the *Catechism* (2363): "The spouses' union achieves the twofold end of marriage: the good of the spouses themselves and the transmission of life. [...] The conjugal love of man and woman thus stands under the twofold obligation of fidelity and fecundity." If one of these two is missing, our moral compass informs us there is something wrong, because intercourse is being reduced to a means of self-indulgence and pleasure-seeking—something we called "lust" before. "Sexual pleasure is morally disordered when sought for itself, isolated from its procreative and unitive purposes," says the *Catechism* (2351).

This may happen not only inside a marriage, but also outside a marriage. In either case, sexuality is "taking" without "giving." When this happens outside a marriage, it takes advantage of the other person for selfish needs without giving the other person a lifelong commitment of love. The *Catechism* (2361) says about sexuality, "It is realized in a truly human way only if it is an integral part of the love by which a man and woman commit themselves totally to one another until death." In contrast, extramarital sexual intercourse is either fornication or adultery. It is fornication if neither person is married, and it is adultery if at least one of the persons is married.

These are not just moral verdicts falling from the sky. They come with our human nature. When we violate human nature, we will soon see detrimental effects, because we starve human nature in its need for love (fidelity) and new life (fecundity). Even tomatoes thrive healthily if we treat them according to their nature by watering them and giving them the right nutrients; it is the same with human nature's sexuality. It is becoming more and more clear what happens when marriage and procreation are taken out of the picture. Janet E. Smith poses a pertinent question:

> What can we say about the moral sexual health of our society? What does the fact that 68% of African-American babies are born out of wedlock suggest? The figure is now 22% in the white community and rapidly growing. This figure, of course, would be higher if it were not for the one and a half million abortions a year. One of two marriages is going to end in divorce. AIDS is decimating some portions of our population. Are there any hints here that we are violating nature, acting irrationally, failing to live in accord with reality? Are our tomato plants thriving?

Some have argued that this new trend is connected with the "sexual revolution" which has aimed to liberate humanity from any sexual restraints. Its origin can probably be traced back to Sigmund Freud, who made us believe that we suffer psychologically when we suppress our sexual desires. He did not discover the lust of the flesh, of course—Adam and Eve did, long before him—but he glorified it, teaching us that we must be liberated from old taboos regarding sex. As a consequence, we have become a culture ruled by Viagra, prostitution, pornography, sexual abuse, and rape. As Peter Kreeft points out, this so-called "revolution" has only led to growing numbers of children who are sexually abused and women who are beaten, abandoned, or raped by men who do not want to hear about self-control and who consider every subject they meet as a mere object for their own use or abuse.

Gabriele Kuby, a German sociologist, has produced a masterly book that documents the deliberate and systematic destruction of the innocence of children, especially in the West, through an intense sexualization process by government-sponsored educational programs. The central thesis of her book is that human freedom is being destroyed in the name of freedom—that is, by a mad quest for absolute freedom, which is leading to a new form of totalitarianism. More than ever, we need to reaffirm that sex belongs to the domain of marriage, monogamy, love, and fidelity; that sex is for life, not only for fun; that the taming of the sex drive and the proper direction of its energies are necessary conditions for social stability and long-term human happiness. On the other hand, as long as society keeps telling parents, and parents keep showing their teenage daughters and friends, that there is no difference between being sexy and being beautiful, the character formation of our next generation will be in jeopardy. Of course, there is a similar story for the macho image of teenage boys. They need to be shown that being a strong boy is not the same as acting in a macho way.

This is where we need a sound moral compass. Morality is not ruled by passions; instead, passions need to be governed by morality, before they destroy ourselves and our society. Desires, feelings, emotions—sometimes called "the passions"—all have an important place in married life. But because sexual passion is the strongest and most attractive of all passions, it is also the most addictive and the most blinding. Therefore, there is no more powerful undermining of our moral knowledge and our moral life than the sexual revolution. The day is coming when more and more people damaged by the false promises of the sexual revelation will find themselves desperately seeking a moral promise that they can trust.

In the meantime, this so-called revolution keeps doing its work. It affects almost every aspect of morality and has contributed greatly to an increase in sex outside marriage, in unwed pregnancies, abortion, single parenthood, cohabitation, divorce, poverty, the exploitation of women, and declining marriage rates. It has even affected the way new, young, and vulnerable family members see themselves. Let us demonstrate this in the case of women in particular—the beautiful sex—by following the thoughts of writer and speaker Emily Stimpson. She describes a beautiful girl as a woman who is lovely in body and soul. Her loveliness starts on the inside and is reflected on the outside. Her beauty is about much more than the sum of her parts, so she chooses to *veil* some of her parts. Eve's fig leaves were intended to help Adam see her as a subject, instead of an object; they were intended to protect her from being taken and used.

True, character formation unfolds at home, but home is surrounded by a specific society and culture, which tells us nowadays that being "sexy" should become the goal for the female gender. As they grow up, women are forced to believe that being sexy and being beautiful are the same thing—but they are not. Each quality actually counteracts the other: "sexy" unveils all that beauty veils. It puts everything on display like an object in a store window, changing subjects into objects, unless we decide to turn the tide. We are not animals; a peacock male displays and exposes everything at his disposal to attract any female available, but Adam discovered in Paradise that no animal was his match.

Needless to say, this situation calls for self-discipline based on morality. Unlimited searching for pleasure makes people over-dosed, over-loaded, over-eaten, and over-sexed, opening the gate-way for addictions such as pornography and prostitution. We need to learn how to keep pleasure within its healthy, natural limits, exerting control over excess by self-discipline—a skill which must be learned as early as possible, since it is not inborn. Hopefully, our parents started us on this path when they taught us delayed gratification—choosing a delayed, larger reward over an immediate, smaller reward. Training our desires is like training our muscles—initially fatigued, we become stronger over time with frequent exercise.

Here lies an important task for parents: parenting. More and more parents think that parenting is a matter of giving children a vote. The concepts of authority and hierarchy have become suspect. However, when parents give up their parental authority, they set their children adrift, for children need firm guidance. When their parents don't provide it, they look to peers or the internet. As Dr. Leonard Sax, MD, puts it, "Legitimate authority establishes a stable moral universe for children." The psychologist Diana Baumrind has found that the most effective parents, as measured by long-term outcomes, are those who are both strict and loving. But she has also found that many of today's parents don't understand that "strict" and "loving" can and must go together, so their children end up drifting.

In order to prepare ourselves for life, we need to learn how to control our appetites and emotions. Life is not always fun and pleasure. The more one is prepared for that inevitable fact of life, the lower the chances are of falling into a depression, easily followed by an addiction. However, the tools of self-control and self-discipline have to be mastered, and you have a better chance in life if your parents have already helped you and taught you to acquire them. No one likes discipline, but the reality is that we do not live in a hedonistic paradise. As the philosopher Hugh J. McCann puts it, this world is not a place in which comfort and convenience are maximized, in which everyone has an electrode implanted to cause intense euphoria and ecstasy in the limbic system with a simple push of the button.

Without a doubt, pleasure plays an important role in our lives. If eating food and having sex did not stimulate feelings of pleasure and reward, we would die out. Our brains are wired to ensure that we will repeat life-sustaining activities by associating those activities with pleasure or reward. The limbic system, which contains the brain's reward circuit, lies on both sides of the thalamus, right under the cerebrum, and links a number of brain structures that control and regulate our ability to feel pleasure. The limbic system is activated when we perform pleasurable activities. It has a dopamine-rich area, which is an intersection where all pleasure-related behaviors meet.

Whenever this reward circuit is activated, the brain notes that something "great" is happening that needs to be remembered, and motivates us to do it again and again, without thinking about it. This is what happens when people become addicted to sex, gambling, and porn. Pornography, for instance, may start in a rather harmless way but then gets progressively worse. The brain adjusts to overwhelming surges in dopamine by producing less dopamine or by reducing the number of receptors that can receive those signals, so the addict seeks more vile images to produce the initial effect. An overstimulation of this system produces the euphoric effects sought by people who abuse sex, stimulating them to increasingly repeat the behavior. As a result, the impact of dopamine on the reward circuit can become abnormally low, and the ability to experience any pleasure is reduced. Over time, if abuse continues, pleasurable activities become less pleasurable, and more abuse becomes necessary for abusers to simply feel "normal." Once the behavior is triggered, it is hard to counteract the dopamine reward system. The shortest road to addictions is to dull oneself and nurse one's pleasures. This is when pleasure becomes lust. Only self-discipline can counteract this.

Training in self-discipline is part of our uniquely human features of rationality and morality. However, it has to battle with the pleasure impulses of the limbic system that we share with the animal world. Training in self-discipline cannot start early enough. Children who do not learn the meaning of the word "no" will be at the mercy of impulses and desires they do not know how to control. They turn into spoiled and demanding little tyrants who have not learned that there is a higher authority—at first, the authority of parents, but ultimately the authority of the natural law. Not having learned the meaning of constraint could scar them for life.

This holds also, or particularly, for our sexuality. If we do not learn how to curb our sexual appetites, we may never be able to end up in a stable, enjoyable, and rewarding marriage—good for the two spouses themselves, for their offspring, and ultimately for society. We have to be prepared for marriage, as marriage is rewarding but not easy. No matter how much we love our spouses, we will have our differences; these may be as minor as where to squeeze the toothpaste tube or as serious as having different religious convictions. Since divorce was made easier by civil law, the number of divorces has been on the rise. It used to be rather common for parents to have four or more children; nowadays it is rather common for children to have four or more parents. Pope Francis, in his *The Joy of Love* (113), says,

> We have to realize that all of us are a complex mixture of light and shadows. The other person is much more than the sum of the little things that annoy me. Love does not have to be perfect for us to value it. The other person loves me as best they can, with all their limits, but the fact that love is imperfect does not mean that it is untrue or unreal.

Can we turn the tide? Yes, we need to make marriage a love story again. But love is a two-way street. On the one hand, it means

"Someone is there for you." On the other hand, it also means "You are there for someone else." The very essence of love demands that we give it away, for love cannot exist in the same space as possessiveness and selfishness. St. Thomas Aquinas explains that "it is more proper to charity to desire to love than to desire to be loved." Love only prospers in a marriage where there is commitment and fidelity. Without these, love is an empty shell. As Pope Francis puts it in *The Joy of Love* (164), "We love the other person for who they are, not simply for their body. Although the body ages, it still expresses that personal identity that first won our heart." Perhaps many adults nowadays are as much in need of "sex education" as the younger generation to learn that love is more than sex. The famous song "Love Hurts" makes it clear that real love does hurt, because it is unconditional.

More than ever, we need to counteract the effects of the "sexual revolution." At the moment "love" is detached from marriage, it becomes a menace and turns into "lust." This same love—or actually lust—makes people leave their families and neglect their moral duties. Love can create practically incurable wounds when it is refused, trampled upon, or not returned. Love is like a beautiful river that turns into a menacing torrent once it exceeds its bounds. Yet, this very love urges people to make one of the most important decisions in life: the decision to marry, to take another's side for good, to share every part of life from now on with our significant other. In fact, love is the only valid reason to do so. Otherwise, having the other person always around will gradually become more and more of a nuisance.

Therefore, the word *love* is no longer sufficient in itself; another word is needed, namely the word *fidelity*. However, fidelity means more than what we usually think it does. The *Catechism* (2365) says, "Fidelity expresses constancy in keeping one's given word." Most people believe in the idea of a "soul mate," of someone who is always there for them, ready to meet their every need. But many forget that they should be there for their soul mate as well—not "as long as we both shall *love*" but "as long as we both shall *live*." And children naturally and usually become an expression of this love, the tangible fruit of a life-long love—a safe cradle for new life.

3

Contraception

Contraception is probably as old as humanity—a product of Sin in Paradise, so to speak. It tries to prevent con-ception with contra-ception. Many centuries ago, Arab camel drivers learned to apply contraception to their camels by placing a little stone in their uterus, which prevented these camels from becoming pregnant so that they would be better able to handle long journeys through the desert. Many other tools have been used to prevent pregnancy from early ages on—not only for camels, but also for human beings. Five different papyri, all dating from between 1900 and 1100 BC, provide recipes for contraceptive preparations. There is nothing new under the Sun.

Obviously, the more we know about the process of conception, the more opportunities we have to disrupt this natural process. Recently, we have come to know a lot about the biology of conception and the events leading up to it and following it. As a result, the contraception industry is booming. Let us briefly discuss the main events related to conception.

The Events Surrounding Conception

For procreation to take place, it is necessary that men produce sperm cells with a single set of 23 chromosomes and that women release egg-cells, again with a single set of 23 chromosomes. For men, starting in puberty, the production of sperm cells happens in their testes, continuously through the rest of their lives. Women go through a different process. Starting in puberty, but ending during menopause, a woman goes through a cycle of some 28 days during which one of her ovaries releases usually one egg containing an egg-cell. This release is called ovulation. Hormones such as estrogen and progesterone are an important part of this menstrual cycle; a rise in estrogen surrounds ovulation, whereas a rise in progesterone feeds the lining of the uterus.

Women are born with all the egg cells they are ever going to have, and they do not make any new cells during their lifetime. They were born with approximately 2,000,000 egg cells in their ovaries, but about 11,000 of them die every month prior to puberty (dying cells are a common phenomenon in human biology; every day, for example, some 500 billion blood cells are eliminated by programmed cell death, in order to offset their continual production in the bone marrow). As a teenager, a woman has only some 400,000 remaining eggs, and from that point on, approximately 1,000 eggs are destined to die each month. This phenomenon is independent of any hormone production, birth control pills, pregnancies, nutritional supplements, or even health or lifestyle. As Dr. Sherman J. Silber puts it: "Whenever the woman runs out of her supply of eggs, her ovaries cease to make estrogen, and she goes through menopause."

During a few days preceding ovulation, the lining of her uterus becomes enlarged and thickened with blood in order to prepare the possibility of fertilization. If the egg cell is not fertilized, both the egg and the lining are shed about 14 days after the start of ovulation. This discharge, called menstruation or a menstrual period, lasts on average five days. During the next nine days, a new lining grows in the uterus, after which the process of ovulation starts all over again. The entire cycle lasts, on average, 28 days, but may slightly vary.

A woman can only become pregnant if she has sexual intercourse around the time the egg is released. Sperm cells can live for as long as 6 days, so if there is intercourse between 5 days before the release of the egg and 1 day after, a sperm cell will be able to fertilize the egg. When a sperm cell, with one set of 23 chromosomes, and an egg cell, also with a single set of 23 chromosomes, come together, they fuse their chromosomes and start a new organism with 23 *pairs* of chromosomes. Father and mother each contribute a half set of their chromosomes—one of each pair—so that their child ends up with a complete set of 23 pairs.

In human beings, the egg cell is fertilized soon after ovulation, while it is still in the upper portion of the oviduct on its way to the uterus. Once the egg cell has been fertilized by a sperm cell, the development of a new organism starts its course. What is present at fertilization is an entire new human being, even though it is yet a single cell. This is the most complicated cell in the universe, for it contains within itself almost all the information that is needed for this human being to develop into a mature adult. This is a process of staggering complexity of which we only understand tiny parts. Adults possess a total of approximately 10^{14} (100 trillion) cells, consisting of more than 200 differentiated cell types. Starting from a single cell—the fertilized egg cell—all these diverse cell types have to be produced and organized into tissues and organs. The fertilized egg cell starts this process with the rapid proliferation of new cells through cell division or cleavage—in an exponential fashion, from one to two, from two to four, from four to eight, from eight to sixteen, and so forth, up to 100 trillion.

Approximately 9 to 10 days after ovulation, the growing fertilized egg cell implants in the uterine lining. Once embedded, the developing baby—often referred to as an *embryo* and, later, as a *fetus*—goes through intense basic growth, launching the development of the brain, spinal cord, heart, and gastrointestinal tract. In nine months, the baby is ready to leave the mother's womb and start a life of its own without a direct connection to the mother.

When Does Human Life Begin?

When calling an organism "human," most people have two very different things in mind. On the one hand, the word "human" can be a descriptive qualification in terms of biology; an organism is called human because it came from human beings, its DNA is human, its developmental path is human, its anatomy and physiology are human, and it belongs to the human race. This version of the word "human" is descriptive in the same way as the word "normal" can describe what we consider the norm, the average, or the standard.

On the other hand, the word "human" also has a moral or ethical connotation. In that specific sense, it is not of a descriptive but prescriptive nature. Calling a being "human," in this prescriptive sense, means that it meets the criteria for human qualifications, including human rights, and therefore deserves human protection and merits to be treated as a human being. In this context, to think differently would be "inhuman." This version of "human" is prescriptive in the same way as the world "normal" can also prescribe what is considered normal versus what is deemed "abnormal." Moral prescriptions are not descriptions, but they tell us what we owe others—our duties—and what others owe us—our rights.

So when we ask when human life begins, we could be in for some confusion. No wonder that the answers to this question have been manifold. Most people take it as a biological question. Some say that human life does not start until the growing embryo finds its "nest" in the uterus of the mother. Some say that it is not really human until the neural system has developed. Others claim that it only becomes human at the moment of birth, when it starts to breathe on its own. Of course, one could counter that it is human, in a purely biological sense, from the moment of conception on, since it is the offspring of two human beings and carries human DNA.

However, all these different positions cannot do full justice to the moral issue of human life. Morality is about absolute, universal, timeless, and objective moral laws and values, as we discussed earlier. The problem with moral prescriptions is that they do not coincide with biological descriptions, for there is nothing absolute about biological considerations; biological criteria are relative, whereas moral criteria are absolute. In general, biological criteria do not qualify as moral criteria. We cannot derive moral guidelines from biological descriptions. The fact of biological development does not mean that there is also a development in human dignity and human rights. The fact that some people are richer than others, or more intelligent than others, does not mean that we ought to value them differently in a moral sense. In a similar way, if some unborn babies are more developed than others, this does not give them more human dignity.

Nevertheless, the value of human life—a moral issue—has often been based on the use of biological criteria, such as the extent of cerebral activity. This is a kind of quasi-moral argument that would go along the following lines: The more cerebral activity there is, the more value a human being has, and therefore, the more rights it has and the more protection it deserves. Others would rather choose viability as the main biological norm to determine the human dignity of an unborn child—the more viable, the more human. This suggests that a potential human being is not necessarily an actual human being. If this were true, we should ask where the dividing line would be between a potential and an actual human being. Even if a potential human being is not as valuable as an actual human being, wouldn't it be at least "almost" as valuable? Clearly, the biological criteria adduced here are biological descriptions and do not ipso facto qualify as moral prescriptions. They are relative, not absolute criteria, and thus become moving targets. So they make only for quasi-moral arguments.

Someone who showed us very clearly that relative criteria cannot qualify as absolute moral claims was President Abraham Lincoln, who applied this to the contentious moral issue of slavery. His point was that all the answers slave holders might come up with to defend their "moral claims" use relative criteria: It is considered morally right to enslave people with a darker skin color or a lower intelligence. If that were so, someone with a lighter skin or higher intelligence would in turn have the "moral right" to enslave these slave holders, because those criteria are entirely relative. As Lincoln said, "By this rule, you are to be slave to the first man you meet, with a fairer skin than your own. […] By this rule, you are to be slave to the first man you meet, with an intellect superior to your own." This is a serious warning for those who confuse moral principles with non-moral criteria.

A similar argument can be used for the moral value of human life. This value cannot be based on biological standards, since those are per definition relative, not absolute. In other words, the moral quality of human life cannot be based on biological criteria. It cannot be quantified and measured on a scale; it does not depend on the degree of cerebral activity, and the like. We cannot use relative standards of intelligence, viability, maturity, health, or fitness to measure or judge the absolute moral value of human life, its human dignity, and its human rights. Biological standards are of a quantitative nature and thus can be put on a scale, but moral standards are of a qualitative nature and cannot be rated or ranked. They are universal, absolute, timeless, objective, and nonnegotiable.

Put differently, we cannot use biological criteria to make a moral decision—something like "the adult is more important than the unborn baby," or "the value of an independent human life outweighs the value of a dependent human life," or "a full-grown person is worth more than a growing fetus," or "a full-grown brain is worth more than a brain in development," or "a life in the womb has fewer rights than a life in the cradle," or "a perfect embryo is worth more than an imperfect embryo," and the list could go on and on. Human status, human rights, and human dignity are not man-made but God-given. Being of human descent is all that counts; one cannot earn or forfeit one's humanity and the rights or duties that come with it. What happens during conception is that human persons, the parents, bring new embodied images of God into our world.

When the law professor Hadley Arkes asks why the offspring of *Homo sapiens* in the womb should be anything less than a human being, he answers the question this way:

> It doesn't speak? Neither do deaf mutes. It has yet no arms or legs? Well, other people lose arms or legs in the course of their lives without losing their standing as human beings in receiving the protections of the law. The upshot here is that there is nothing one could cite to disqualify the child in the womb as a human being that would not apply to many people walking about well outside the womb. Once again, there is no appeal to faith or beliefs. One doesn't have to be Catholic or religious in order to understand this argument—and that has been precisely the argument of the Church, that this is a matter that turns on the moral reasoning of the natural law.

Consequently, there is no such thing as "growing in humanity." There is growth of a biological body, but there is no growth of moral rights. Each human being is a person with body and soul; there is no such thing as a disembodied soul or a soul-less human body. Each human being, regardless of age, is genetically and spiritually the same human being at every stage of life's journey, in spite of changes in appearance. It is a *human* being from the very beginning—perhaps not complete yet, but in the same way as children and teenagers are still incomplete adults. At the moment of conception, the new being could essentially say "I am a boy" or "I am a girl." From fertilization on, life's journey is a continuum, so there is no such thing as a "pre-human stage" in this process. Some might say that personhood is a legal construct, not something found in nature—suggesting that a living entity becomes a person, and is therefore entitled to a right to life, when the law says it is a person. David Carlin responds, "But this means that a dog is a person if the law says it is, and that a baby is not a person till its first birthday—if the law decrees that. Nor is X a person if the government of this or that society declares X a non-person." That would be a confusion of natural law with civil law.

Nevertheless, the process from conception on stirs endless debates, ranging from minor to major. Is there any reason to think that the human embryo is not *alive*? It is clear that the embryo can die, but since only living beings can die, the embryo must be living. Is there any reason to think that this living embryo is *not* human? Since the embryo arises from a human mother and a human father, what species could it be other than human? As a matter of fact, the newly-conceived human embryo is biologically and genetically one of us. The embryo is not a part of the mother (as is obvious when the embryo is growing in a petri dish), but is rather made from part of the mother (her egg cell) and part of the father (his sperm cell). It is hard to deny that, from conception on, the growing embryo is a new human being, distinct from both the father and the mother.

What has made the discussion even murkier is the fact that for a long time, some biologists claimed that a human embryo, during its development in the womb, repeats the process of evolution—from a simple to a more complex organism, from fish to man. Indeed, during embryological development, we often do find intermediary stages of what were once final stages in more primitive animals. Human embryos, for instance, early on develop gill pouches just like fish, although they never become real gills, and the human cerebrum develops last. Human embryos also grow a layer of downy hair that they shed after about thirty-five weeks of gestation.

However, all of this does not mean that human embryos are retracing the evolutionary history of humanity as they develop. The human embryo never has real gills in any sense of the word. The fanciful notion of such human gills is based upon the presence of six alternating ridges and grooves in the neck-region of the human embryo. While similar arches do give rise to gills in certain aquatic vertebrates such as fish, their development in mammals has nothing to do with gills or even breathing. In humans and other mammals, these arches and pouches develop into part of the face, and its jaws (the first arch; a faulty closing of this arch would cause a cleft palate), muscles of facial expression (the second arch), some endocrine glands (the third and fourth arches), and the larynx (the sixth arch), whereas the fifth arch in fact disappears. Nevertheless, the erroneous idea that an embryo repeats evolution and starts with something like a fish stage has infiltrated general thinking. It can still be found in outdated biology textbooks used at some schools and colleges.

Even when we use different terms such as embryo, fetus, or unborn baby, in all such instances we are referring to steps in one long, continuous developmental growth process that comes forth from two other human beings, and starts with a fertilized egg cell outfitted with its own human chromosomes and human DNA. What remains the same during the entire process of adding, replacing, and losing cells is the person's identity, the person's embodied soul. Humans have the capacity to undergo biological change without losing their identity. Although our bodies change constantly, we ourselves do not—that is, our personal identity remains the same, and so does our moral status. In a certain sense, the body is something we *have*, but also something we *are*.

Because of this, a human being cannot *become* human. It *is* already human from its very beginning; human life is a journey that does not start "halfway." A woman is either pregnant or she is not—she cannot be "half-pregnant." From this follows an important conclusion: during its development, a new human being does not become human at a certain point, nor does it turn more and more human, but rather it *is* uniquely human at every stage of its growth. As Pope Francis put it in his apostolic exhortation *Evangelii Gaud-*

ium, "A human being is always sacred and inviolable, in any situation and at every stage of development. Human beings are ends in themselves and never a means of resolving other problems." Each one of us is a unique human being from the moment of conception.

Since development in the womb is a continuum, embryos do not spontaneously transform into human beings at the moment their senses start to function, any more than they spontaneously transform into human beings at the moment their hearts start to beat, or their limbs start to move, or their brains begin to function—each of which occurs at different time points along the child's normal path of growth and development. To use an analogy, the monarch butterfly goes through dramatic changes from egg to caterpillar, to pupa, and finally to a mature butterfly, but it remains a member of the species *Danaus plexippus* all the way along. One cannot say that the caterpillar is *not* a member of that species. One and the same entity may go through various appearances, but it remains the same entity. In spite of all the changes a human embryo will go through, it will never change into a banana, because it has a body with a human soul.

Strangely enough, some people think of human rights as if they were entitlements that the government gives us. True, we gain entitlements as we age—US citizens can drive a car at sixteen, can vote at eighteen, can buy alcohol at twenty-one. But we cannot apply this kind of reasoning to human rights. Protection of a human being is not a conditional legal entitlement, but an unconditional moral right. It does not progress with age, but is rooted in the fact that we are dealing with a human being from the very beginning. There is no gradualism when it comes to human rights; killing a twenty-week-old is not worse than killing a ten-week-old or a thirty-week-old unborn baby. There is a fundamental difference between the moral right to life and the entitlements we were given to vote or drive.

The neuroscientist and bioethicist Fr. Tadeusz Pacholczyk uses the thalidomide drama of the late 1950s and early 1960s to clarify that, if it were true that women are not pregnant with a human being prior to eight weeks of age, then taking a drug like thalidomide would not raise any concerns, since no human being would be present to be harmed by the drug anyway. But it is well known that the most drug-susceptible period during pregnancy is the first tri-mester, specifically between the 4th and the 7th week of gestation. Apparently, each human being arises at fertilization and consists as a biological continuum thereafter. Fr. Pacholczyk also uses another analogy:

> Even atheists can see how a bald eagle's eggs ought to be protected; it's not a religious question at all. If bald eagles are valuable (in this case, for pragmatic reasons of conservation), then it is right and fitting to protect them at all stages of their existence. The same logic holds for humans, who are valuable not for pragmatic but for intrinsic reasons.

In other words, upon fusion with a sperm cell, the egg cell as egg no longer exists, and a human being—outfitted with his or her own soul and genetically distinct from his or her mother and father—starts a new life's journey. I realize, for instance, that I myself started at one point in my life as a fertilized egg cell and that at some point in time I will be dead. It is my very "self" that connects all these stages of my life as one long continuum. That is the unity between body and soul we talked about earlier. No matter whether cells in my body keep being replaced, my personal identity stays the same. About 98 percent of the atoms of the adult human body, including those found in the brain and nervous system, are replaced in about every two years.

Some have argued that this view is not in line with what Thomas Aquinas asserted. Aquinas distinguishes three different souls: Plants have a vegetative soul, with growth, metabolism, and procreation; animals have a sensitive soul, with locomotion and perception; and human beings have an intellective soul, with reason and intellect. These are "nested" in the sense that anything that has a higher degree of soul also has all of the lower degrees. All living things, including plants, grow, nourish themselves, and reproduce. Animals not only have those activities, but they also move and perceive. Humans also use reason and intellect, but do all of the above as well.

Aquinas seems to also apply these distinctions to the develop-ment of a human person in the womb. This has led some people to conclude that an unborn baby is a mere vegetable in its first stage, a mere animal in its second, and finally a human being in its third. This may contain an element of truth, as embryology confirms that metabolism and growth appear before the sensory and neural system develop, and finally the cerebral system matures. But we cannot automatically conclude from this that the unborn baby goes through three different types of souls.

Was Aquinas wrong on this issue? It is a very controversial question. Some say that he was deceived by the limited knowledge ancients had about embryology, and thus came up with the idea of a delayed hominization. The underlying thought is that a child has a human soul when it has a human "form"—that is, when the child "looks" human. But "looks" can be very deceiving. In contrast, others say that Aquinas does speak of a *virtus formativa*, which is what directs the human embryo's development toward the appropriate form, its soul. Just as DNA provides a blueprint for the body's development, the *virtus formativa* contains every feature of the developing body, but contains it "virtually" or "potentially," rather than actually. Nowadays, we could translate it this way: Human DNA gives the unborn baby a human form, even when it may not look human yet.

Then there is a third group of people who say that Aquinas only claims that the nutritive and sentient elements of humans are subsumed under the intellective soul. Aquinas uses a slightly misleading terminology when he tells us that the intellective soul "contains *virtually* whatever belongs to the sensitive soul of brute animals, and to the nutritive souls of plants." Compare this with water (H_2O): It contains oxygen (O_2) and hydrogen (H_2), but it is no longer oxygen and hydrogen; oxygen and hydrogen are not actually in the substance water, but they are there "virtually," i.e. by their power [*virtus*].

Whatever view we take, the fact remains that the embryo is not a mere vegetable in its first stage, a mere animal in its second, and finally a human being in its third. Rather, the human soul must *always*, at any stage, organize the body if development is to be determined from within. Without a human soul, there would be no development of a human being. A human embryo does not become "animated," as some believe, at a certain moment after conception, but is already animated during the entire process. The embryo is a human being from the very beginning, as it goes through the entire process any human being goes through. Plants, for instance, do not go through such a process, because they do not have a human soul. An unborn human is and remains a human being all the way through.

An Assessment of Contraception

The previous considerations have serious consequences for the way we look at contraception. There are many misconceptions about contraception, so we need to create some clarity in this discussion.

The first problem with contraception is that most contraceptives affect certain steps in the process that a human being goes through in its earliest stages of development. Pharmaceutical companies often make it look as though their contraceptives only affect the release of eggs and/or the mobility of sperm cells *before* conception can occur. But usually they also, or only, affect the further development of a *fertilized* egg cell before or during implantation in the uterine wall. Since a fertilized egg cell is a human being from the moment of conception, we could call such contraceptives abortifacients. Let us keep the terminology straight: Whereas a contraceptive prevents human life *before* it begins, an abortifacient acts *after* human life has begun, and thus produces a micro-abortion.

The late obstetrician Dr. J.C. Willke, makes no bones about it:

> But we are told that pregnancy doesn't begin until implantation and that any medication or object which prevents that planting is in fact a contraceptive and will "prevent pregnancy." What has happened has been a redefinition of the terms used. They now tell us that "pregnancy" does not begin until one week after fertilization, the time of implantation. This has fooled untold numbers of people, including many doctors.

How were we fooled? In the early 1960s, officials from the American College of Obstetrics and Gynecology teamed up with the US Food and Drug Administration and redefined the word "conception." They said that "conception" would no longer be the time of union of sperm cell and egg cell, but rather the time, one week later, when this new human becomes implanted inside the lining of the mother's womb. As a consequence, the difference between contraceptives and abortifacients was obliterated. However, whereas diaphragms and condoms are barrier forms of contraception and do not involve abortion, the most common Birth Control Pill does more than prevent ovulation and thicken the cervical mucus, as it also affects the lining of the womb, making it more hostile to implantation of an already fertilized egg. We have here another attempt at redefining key terms in the discussion.

Another common device, the IUD or intrauterine device, also primarily functions to prevent implantation of the tiny developing human being. Then there is Plan B and Ella for "emergency contraception"—better known as the "morning-after pill." Both of them, but Ella specifically, are designed to prevent the already-conceived human being from implanting in the lining of the uterus, thus causing an early abortion. Nothing could demonstrate this better than the fact that Ella is marketed to be used up to five days after intercourse! That is definitely later than a "morning-after." Further "research" is probably aimed at extending that period of time. This puts us on a slippery slope. Once an abortifacient is called a "contraceptive," everybody is being fooled.

A second problem with contraception is that most contraceptives have serious medical side effects. The World Health Organization has placed the estrogen-progestogen pill on its list of Group 1 carcinogens—the most toxic rating it can impose, together with tobacco and asbestos. As a matter of fact, hormonal contraceptives have been tied to strokes, heart attacks, lupus, inflammatory bowel disease, reduced immunity, and increased susceptibility to sexually transmitted diseases. It also has been found that women who take oral contraceptives are twice as likely to develop cervical cancer, and twenty percent more likely to develop breast cancer than women who never took the Pill. No wonder, then, that there have been recent lawsuits against the pharmaceutical industry. Merck recently agreed to pay $100 million to 3,800 claimants who declared that one of its contraceptives had caused heart attacks, blood clots, and strokes. Bayer also settled for $1.6 billion to claims about blood clots and gallbladder damage.

Nevertheless, due to a well-oiled and heavily-funded public relations campaign of the pharmaceutical industry, the Pill has been heralded as an important tool for women's "health" by plainly ignoring its side effects. They made sure it would become a "sacred cow." The chemist who created the birth control pill, Carl Djerassi envisioned in 1970 that "politics, rather than science, would play the dominant role in shaping the future of human birth control." How right he was! And three months before he died in 2015, he predicted that by the year 2050 "separation between sex and reproduction will be 100 percent," thus making sex a merely recreational issue for those who consider themselves liberated women.

But instead of liberating women, the Pill has placed them at severe risk of illness. As Dr. Marguerite R. Duane, of Georgetown University School of Medicine, puts it, "The pill is the only drug that was developed to be given to a woman who was healthy to create a diseased state." The Pill has also caused a breakdown of the nuclear family and thus an increase in domestic poverty. According to the US Census Bureau, 40% of children raised by single mothers are living in poverty, compared to 8% of children raised by married parents. A broken family life is considered one of the best predictors of poverty. The Pill may not be the main cause of this development, but it is certainly an important contributing factor.

Even if the previous problems did not apply, there is still a moral problem with *all* forms of contraception, including condoms and sterilization. There is an important moral rule that says: not everything that is thinkable or possible in a biological sense is also permissible in a moral sense. It is the Church's teaching that sexuality must be open to the transmission of life, otherwise sex becomes a mere means to pleasure, and nothing more—"recreational sex," in modern terminology. The Church teaches that sexual intercourse was designed by God to allow humanity to participate in the creation of new life via an act of love. This is not just a Catholic viewpoint; until the Conference of Lambeth in 1930, all Christian dominations condemned artificial contraception. But times have changed…

Currently, 99% of Catholic obstetricians, gynecologists, and family practitioners prescribe contraceptives, and either perform or make referrals for sterilization. As medical doctors, they certainly know what *can* be done, but apparently not what *ought* to be done. They know more about biology than about morality, because the latter is usually not taught at medical schools, which makes them think that everything biologically possible is morally permissible. It is worth quoting here the prophetic words of Archbishop Charles Chaput of Philadelphia: "There will be no renewal of America without renewal of the Catholic Church, and no renewal of the Catholic Church without renewal of the Catholic family, and no renewal of the Catholic family without a bold proclamation of the sacred truths regarding the transmission of human life." We might as well add to this that there will be no renewal of our nation without the renewal of our medical doctors.

Since the body is not a machine but rather the expression of the person, the principles of the *Theology of the Body* teach us that we should never harm or alter a major, healthy, functioning part of the human body. This is not "new" theology; almost two millennia ago, around AD 200, St. Clement of Alexandria made this moral admonition: "Because of its divine institution for the propagation of man, the seed is not to be vainly ejaculated, nor is it to be damaged, nor is it to be wasted." Yet that is exactly what is happening. Both contraception and sterilization attack and disrupt our reproductive systems while being deceptively advertised and promoted as "health care." But this form of health care has nothing to do with health, and actually results in very unhealthy consequences.

Does rejection of contraceptives mean a marriage ought to lead to unlimited conceptions whenever they happen to occur? Not at all. What the Church does teach is that all sexual acts must be open to the transmission of new life. She does not teach that conception must occur every time a couple have sex, nor does she teach that infertile couples (infertile through no fault of their own) should not have sexual intercourse. The *Catechism* (2368) says very clearly, "A particular aspect of this responsibility concerns the regulation of procreation. For just reasons, spouses may wish to space the births of their children. It is their duty to make certain that their desire is not motivated by selfishness but is in conformity with the generosity appropriate to responsible parenthood." Elsewhere, the *Cate-*

chism (2399) adds, "The regulation of births represents one of the aspects of responsible fatherhood and motherhood."

The late Fr. Richard M. Hogan expressed this as follows:

> God did not intend that every act of marital love should result in a new human person. There are only a few days in a woman's cycle when a pregnancy is possible. Further, God gave us a mind and a will so that we could cooperate with Him in the creation of a new human person: procreation. Responsible parenthood signifies the virtuous choice made by a married couple either to strive to procreate or to try to avoid conception. [...] God never told married couples when they should make love. That is totally up to the couple. What He does say . . . is that when married couples love, they are to give themselves totally to one another.

This leaves the door open for a different form of birth control or family planning—not through artificial contraceptives, but through what is called *Natural Family Planning* (NFP). Natural Family Planning is the process of abstaining from sexual intercourse during the time a woman is fertile and able to conceive. To determine when ovulation occurs, the woman observes changes that occur within her body.

There are three methods of natural family planning. One is the process of observing changes in cervical mucus, for during ovulation, the mucus becomes stretchy, clear, and slick. The other method is a daily monitoring of the woman's temperature, which will slightly rise during ovulation. A third method monitors urine levels of luteinizing hormone (LH), a hormone produced by the pituitary gland. Although the female body always makes a small amount of LH, it makes much more of it just before ovulation. A blood or urine test can detect this LH surge, which usually happens 1–1½ days before ovulation. These three methods can help couples with family planning. Whereas couples who use contraceptives withhold their fertility from one another, NFP couples practice family planning when they know that they are infertile.

Currently, there is another method in a very far stage of development. It tests for progesterone levels. Progesterone is produced in the ovaries after a mature egg is released. Testing for progesterone is more reliable than using ovulation strips for estrogen and LH, because the presence of these two hormones does not confirm if or when ovulation occurs; sometimes the body can provide signs of ovulation without actually ovulating. Test strips for progesterone would solve this uncertainty and could be used at home. They would present an advantage for women who have irregular or hard-to-read cycles.

NFP should not be confused with the so-called "rhythm method" that our grandmothers may have used. The rhythm method standardizes every woman's cycle to 28 days, with an ovulation on day 14. But not every cycle is of the same length, and some women have irregular cycles. The NFP method, on the other hand, is customized to each woman's individual cycle every month. Women are instructed in how to recognize their signs of fertility. This may also help in finding out why some women have trouble getting pregnant if their fertility period is extremely short. Needless to say, NFP does not cause any side effects, but it does require self-control during the short time of fertility.

All of this having been said, the question may arise as to whether artificial contraception is always wrong in all circumstances. There may be situations when the Principle of Double Effect kicks in: a good effect one intends and an evil effect one does *not* intend. This principle has been applied to situations where rape is involved, for instance. Although there is no way abortion could solve this moral conflict, the Principle of Double Effect might legitimize the use of artificial contraceptives as a way to avoid pregnancy in cases of rape. Under these circumstances, the intention of the woman is not to render her sexual intercourse non-procreative, but to prevent the harmful effect of a sexual attack. Her intention is not contraception, and certainly not intercourse, but self-defense. Obviously, this holds only for contraception used to prevent conception, not to end a conception that has already taken place.

Therefore, it is not so easy to apply this moral argument also to recent cases of the Zika virus, which may lead to birth defects in the unborn baby, such as microcephaly. When life gets hard, we cannot decide which moral rules apply to us and which do not. The use of artificial contraceptives based on the Principle of Double Effect is only morally acceptable if the woman is not intending any sexual intercourse. Sexually active women who use contraceptives to avoid pregnancy can hardly claim that they are engaging in an act of self-defense. Instead, they should avoid pregnancy by abstinence or by the use of natural methods of birth control.

Yet the case has been made that the use of some forms of contraception, such as condoms, would be permissible if there is the intention to prevent a child from being born with a disease such as AIDS or microcephaly. The problem with this moral argument is that the Principle of Double Effect requires more than an intended good effect and a non-intended evil effect. A third requirement of this principle is that the bad effect is not the means for attaining the good effect, for good effects do not justify the use of evil means. In this scenario, the bad effect, contraception, is in fact the very means for attaining the good effect, the prevention of a disease. Besides, many forms of contraception do not simply prevent conception but stop the further development of an already fertilized egg cell after conception has taken place, which moves the discussion to an entirely different level.

Marriage and Procreation

The use of artificial contraceptives is one of the main driving forces behind the current "sexual revolution" because it allows sex at any time with anyone without the "risk" of conception. In turn, the sexual revolution is a major cause of the breakdown of the nuclear family. Thus there is a direct line from artificial contraception to the breakdown of the nuclear family. Once we disconnect procreation from marriage, the nuclear family is at risk. Marriage combined with procreation is the cornerstone of the nuclear family. Although there are situations in a marriage when procreation is not possible or not advisable, procreation is the necessary condition in a marriage for building a nuclear family, as it allows humanity to participate in the creation of new life via an act of love.

Pope John Paul II famously exclaimed, "The family is the basic cell of society. It is the cradle of life and love, the place in which the individual is born and grows." It creates a triangle of love. As G.K. Chesterton put it, "This triangle of truisms, of father, mother and child, cannot be destroyed; it can only destroy those civilizations which disregard it." Chesterton also says, "If a triangle breaks out of its three sides, its life comes to a lamentable end."

As a matter of fact, the nuclear family is the most ancient of human institutions, going back as far as Adam and Eve; it is universal and has an authority. Society's moral infrastructure rests squarely on the foundation of the nuclear family. Dr. Rebecca Peck says in no uncertain terms:

> What about the rising divorce rates and single parenthood? The saddest women I see in medical practice are single women, depressed and exhausted from trying to work and fulfill the role of mother and father. Children are neglected. Poverty and violence are increasing. The traditional family is becoming a thing of the past.

There is strong scientific evidence that children who spend their childhood years with their married biological parents have fewer cognitive, behavioral, and emotional problems than children who did not. Too many children grow up with an absent parent. Do not take this the wrong way: there are perfectly good single parents who raise perfectly fine children. Yet we should not forget that one of the best predictors of poverty is a broken family life.

The *Catechism* (2207) calls the family "the original cell of social life." Families are to society what cells are to a body; they are the basic building blocks. The family is the first place where children learn life's most important lessons. The family is the first place where children find protection and learn the role of being a male or female. None of these "lessons" are inborn; they must be taught and nurtured with tender loving care. As Peter Kreeft remarks, "Societies have survived with very bad political systems and very bad economies, but not without strong families." Families are grounded in the strong bond of a marriage: only if you marry me and stand by me can you count on me to bear and help raise your children. This requires a commitment on both sides—no involvement without commitment.

Character formation may certainly be done in school, but it begins in the family. We cannot expect schools to correct what went wrong in the family on a 24/7 basis. The family is of vital importance in the development of human beings. Pope Francis declared in his *The Joy of Love* (175): "The clear and well-defined presence of both figures, female and male, creates the environment best suited to the growth of the child." As a matter of fact, babies can tell mother from father as early as three weeks after birth. Almost invariably, they make this same distinction, becoming calm in the presence of the mother, aroused and stimulated by the approach of the father. The interactions between infant and father, as between infant and mother, work in either direction and follow a pattern that transcends social class and cultural expectations. The first sentence in Leo Tolstoy's book *Anna Karenina* puts it well: "Happy families are all alike; every unhappy family is unhappy in its own way."

Nowadays, it is especially the role of fathers that needs to be stressed. As children grow toward adulthood, their fathers should play a pivotal role in their development. Children whose fathers help care for them have been shown to be less likely to become violent; they have higher IQs, better impulse control, and better social adaptations—in short, better psychological health. As for the fathers themselves, studies involving inner-city men have shown that fathers also learn from their experience of being a father and are less prone to commit crimes or join gangs when they have children. It has also been shown that fatherhood curbs instincts of aggression. It turns out that testosterone levels drop when men become fathers, and drop even further when they are attentive fathers.

However, it is not only inner-city fathers who tend to be missing in action. Fatherly absence cuts across all socioeconomic lines. Even in privileged homes, fathers can be physically present but emotionally absent, absorbed in work, sports, hobbies, and the like. We often hear that ours is "a society without fathers." Pope Francis underlines this problem in *The Joy of Love* (176): "In our day, the problem no longer seems to be the overbearing presence of the father so much as his absence, his not being there."

The role of fathers is also important in the religious development of a child. The psychotherapist Dr. Greg Popcak explains this as follows: because babies grew inside their mothers, once they are born, they continue to believe that they and their mother are one. As a consequence, in his own words, "Father is experienced by the baby as 'the first other.' Father is 'the world' to the child. If the role of mother is teaching baby how to think about the more private realms of life and home, it is the role of father to represent how 'the world' works." When it comes to prayer, if mom is prayerful, it is seen primarily as a private matter, but if dad is prayerful, the child learns to believe that prayer and faith are public activities that are meant to positively impact the world.

The family is also the place where children learn what is right and wrong—and this process begins at a very simple level. Rushing to the crib every time a child cries may train them to expect instant gratification. Children who do not learn the meaning of the word "no" will be at the mercy of impulses and desires they do not know how to control. They have not learned the meaning of constraint. They have not been disciplined. The word "discipline" sounds rigid and may remind some of spanking, but there are "humane" alternatives to spanking children—grounding them with *timeouts*, for example; soon even the threat of a timeout is effective, if followed by an explanation of why their behavior was bad.

Just as children learn to imitate language and gestures, so they also mimic the moral practices they see at home. The *Catechism* (2207) describes the family as "the community in which, from childhood, one can learn moral values, begin to honor God, and make good use of freedom." Children do need a functional family— it is a *right* that they have and a *duty* that parents owe them. Good role models are essential, making every day a "school day" when it comes to moral development. Children who have never learned to be ashamed of certain behaviors are in real trouble, perhaps for the rest of their lives.

4

Infertility

Marriage is not something that all people are called to strive for, but certainly something all people are invited to consider. It is neither a right nor a duty; no one has the right to get married, and no one has the duty to get married. Not everyone may have children, but everyone does have parents. Therefore, all of us have some connection with parenthood: everyone is either a parent or at least a child of two parents. We may not have children, but we all have ancestors who passed life on to us, their children.

Yet the line of passing on life from generation to generation is sometimes blocked. It is a hard truth in life that some married couples do not have children—not because they do not want to, but because they cannot. Infertility is one of the most painful experiences that some married couples must go through; not only may it create feelings of guilt and shame, it may cause a divide between the two spouses.

In Vitro Fertilization (IVF)

It should not come as a surprise, then, that any technique that could be a solution to infertility would be highly welcomed by such couples. When the first in vitro fertilization was performed, IVF was announced with much fanfare and enthusiasm. It was in 1978 that Dr. Robert Edwards and his colleagues introduced Louise Brown, the first "test tube" baby, to the world. Edwards boasted, "This is the first time we've solved all the problems at once." Now, more than three decades later, IVF is a "standard" procedure. More than four million IVF children populate the globe. In the USA just during one year in 2013, 467 reporting clinics performed nearly 190,773 "cycles" of IVF, resulting in 54,323 deliveries of one or more living infants and 67,996 live born infants. And the numbers keep rising.

Today fertility and infertility have been turned into a lucrative commodity. "Designer" gametes are even sold on the Internet. Infertile couples can expect to pay an average of $66,000 to become pregnant and to have a live-born baby, if IVF succeeds in the first cycle. They will pay an average of $114,000 per delivered baby if treatments are not successful before the sixth cycle. Apparently, fertility is now for sale, making it a very profitable economic enterprise.

Here's what the IVF process basically entails. After surgically removing eggs from the woman's ovaria in drug-induced, super-ovulated cycles, and after collecting sperm cells from the man, usually through masturbation, the egg cells and sperm cells are brought together in a petri dish in the laboratory (*in vitro*). If successful, fertilization takes place in that dish—that is, outside the woman's body, and without any act of sexual union between the two. Next, three or more five-day old embryos are placed in the woman's uterus through a process called "embryo transfer." The remaining embryos are either destroyed or frozen at -320° F in liquid nitrogen, put on hold for possible future implantation or for research purposes.

The results are perplexing. In 2009, a California woman became "Octomom"—giving birth to eight IVF babies—after her doctor was unethical enough to transfer twelve human embryos into her uterus. Then there was the man who made headlines after he "fathered" 150 children (with more on the way), all of whom are half-brothers or half-sisters without knowing about each other— and who will probably never know who their father is. Soon after this, same-sex parenting through IVF was the next development. The request for "designer babies" was next, followed by commercial efforts to market and promote the use of prenatal genetic diagnosis to scan and test chromosomes of IVF embryos, which inevitably leads to elimination of human beings with less-than-desirable genetic traits.

One of the most recent developments in battling infertility is a womb transplant for women who have no uterus because of a hysterectomy or due to a rare congenital disease. Some see this as comparable to something like a kidney transplant—except for the fact, of course, that a womb transplant is not a life-saving surgery like a kidney transplant. The transplanted womb can somehow replace a "surrogate mother." Theoretically, it would be possible to connect the new uterus to the other sexual organs of the woman so that she can become pregnant the natural way. However, the first successful surgery done in Sweden was, not surprisingly, followed by a pregnancy caused by IVF, which shows, again, how fascinated the medical world is with IVF. Normal pregnancies have become "obsolete" in the eyes of many. IVF is now the new fashion to become pregnant.

What Is Wrong with IVF?

Infertility is not a hopeless destiny married couples must learn to live with. The *Catechism* (2293) actually lauds the fight against infertility: "Research aimed at reducing human sterility is to be encouraged, on condition that it is placed 'at the service of the human person, of his inalienable rights, and his true and integral good according to the design and will of God.'"

But is IVF, as a technique to battle infertility, in accordance with this moral guideline? There are several reasons why it is not.

Reason number one is the freezing and discarding of IVF embryos. There is an inevitable surplus of embryos as a result of IVF. If we do not discard them—which is the worst alternative—we still create a dilemma about what to do with the frozen offspring held in "suspended animation." Typically, this leads to human stockpiling. Fr. Tadeusz Pacholczyk speaks of "a kind of 'Wild West,' a lawless frontier where nearly anything goes. […] Because our frozen children have no voice to speak in their own defense, we slip into a mindset that ignores their inherent dignity." In other words, they lead a "shelf life," and may never even leave the "shelf."

Currently, fertility clinics in the USA warehouse more than 500,000 children—labeled as "spares"—stored in high-tech freezers filled with liquid nitrogen. These are the children who are crystallized by-products of the IVF process. Parents can choose to "re-animate" their embryonic children by thawing them, implanting them, and then gestating them. Usually, however, these "spares" end up being abandoned because their parents do not want any more children, or are growing too old to take on a new pregnancy. These freezers become, in essence, liquid-nitrogen orphanages.

Reason number two is that IVF turns sexual procreation into technological production. It creates an "out-of-body" experience for the newborn. It is as though the spouses deny their own bodily (and therefore personal) participation in the conception of their child and opt for a technical alternative. But the human body can never be viewed simply as a source of raw biological material, or as a biological machine. The procedure of "in vitro" fertilization violates the human dignity of the embryo as well as the sacred unity of body and soul. The new child is "produced," treated as a thing, a product. The *Catechism* (2377) gives a good assessment:

> The act which brings the child into existence is no longer an act by which two persons give themselves to one another, but one that entrusts the life and identity of the embryo into the power of doctors and biologists and establishes the domination of technology over the origin and destiny of the human person.

Treating the new child as a mere technological product can have serious consequences. This is clearly seen in the discussion of "designer babies"—children "made to order," children with the "right" intelligence, athletic skills, etc., plus the gender wanted by the parents. If the artificially-conceived embryo is implanted in the womb of another woman—so-called surrogate motherhood—the surrogate mother violates her own dignity by "renting" her body as though it were a machine made for baby-production.

Last but not least, reason number three is that IVF violates the moral rights of the newborn. Rights are what we owe others and what others owe us. They come with the fact that we—even as unborn babies—are human beings in the full sense. Duties and rights go hand in hand, so they have a natural reciprocity: children have the right to be born in the protective shelter of the mother's womb, so parents have the duty to make that happen for their children.

Fr. Pacholczyk Tadeusz elaborates on the moral rights of our new generation as a strong moral argument against IVF. He stresses that our children have the right to be procreated, not produced. They have the right to come into the world in the personal, love-giving embrace of their parents, not in the cold and impersonal glass world of a test tube or Petri dish. They have the right to be uniquely, exclusively, and directly related to the mother and father who bring them into the world. Parents have a moral duty to respect the rights of their children. In contrast, a technique like IVF violates "the child's right to be born of a father and mother known to him and bound to each other by marriage," according to the *Catechism* (2376).

Some might object that parents have a "right" also to have children, even if infertility makes that impossible. However, no one has the right to have children because no one has the duty to have children. The Congregation of the Doctrine of the Faith (CDF) put it well in its 1987 instruction *Donum Vitae*: "The child is not an object to which one has a right, nor can he be considered as an object of ownership: Rather, a child is a gift, 'the supreme gift' and the most gratuitous gift of marriage." This document made it clear that we must not have babies without *sex*, whereas a 1968 document, *Humanae Vitae*, had already explained why we must not have sex without the possibility of *babies*. There are clear harms and evils in the separation of sex from procreation.

Every sexual aberration—fornication, co-habitation, divorce, contraception, or in vitro fertilization—runs the risk of depriving any possible children of the stable, identity-forming environment of the nuclear family, which is their birthright. Children who do not grow in this environment run a serious risk of being wounded or crippled in their identity for the rest of their lives. They may not know who their father is. They may not even know themselves. Mary Ellen Stanford asks the pivotal question: "Can today's adults—so very fixed on trying to find fulfilment through sex—accept the truth that they can survive without sex, but that children cannot thrive without the fullness of Christian marriage?"

These are very serious moral objections to artificial fertilization. Yet the desperation experienced by couples seeking solutions to their infertility often drives them into the arms of IVF specialists who shower them with their seductive marketing techniques. But this need not be. To achieve pregnancy, couples have a choice: they can bypass the reproductive system, as is done in IVF, or they can fix it, as is done in NaPro Technology (Natural Procreative Technology or NPT). The latter is a technology initially developed by Dr. Thomas W. Hilgers. NPT does not aim at artificial fertilization but at *natural* fertilization. It is a medical breakthrough that cooperates with the woman's reproductive cycle to identify what the infertility problem is in order to correct it. It is a fertility-care based medical approach rather than a fertility-control approach to family planning.

NPT has proven to be two to three times more effective than IVF. It teaches the woman to observe and chart cervical discharge, known as a "biomarker," throughout her sexual cycle. With this information, wife and husband know their window of fertile days, especially in case of irregular cycles. This information can also serve as a diagnostic tool to identify any underlying diseases and conditions that cause infertility—for instance, a reduced progesterone production. Whereas IVF "skips over" such problems, NPT can often identify and correct them. Obviously, there are no moral problems with the NPT technology.

But what to do if NPT does not work either? Some have suggested a less controversial alternative to IVF: IUI or Homologous Intrauterine Insemination. The sperm retrieved from the male are then, after a rapid procedure to "capacitate" the sperm-cells, placed inside the woman's reproductive tract with the help of a plastic catheter, so fertilization can take place. Since this procedure appears to "assist" the conjugal act, it may seem a morally acceptable alternative. However, the controversial part is how the semen is being obtained. Since masturbation makes it an act against nature, it has been suggested to use a perforated condom during a marital act, instead of masturbation. Not only is this an awkward solution, but it could still be argued that sperm used in IUI has been intentionally withheld from a marital act. During this marital act, the sperm was not deposited in the wife's body, but in the condom. So the spouses are not the major causes of fertilization; they simply provide the "products," sperm-cells and egg-cell, to be used by "technicians" to arrange fertilization. In other words, IUI is not "assisting" a conjugal act but rather "substituting" for it.

Another problem of the discussion so far is that the inability to get pregnant is often looked at as a women's issue. But statistics show that about 30% are due to the male, and another 30% or so are due to both male and female issues. Two of the main reasons for male infertility are a low sperm cell count or a low sperm cell mobility. The amount of estrogens a man consumes each day through food/water/plastics can have drastic effects on his sperm cell count. And due to nutrient deficiencies, sperm cells are sometimes basically immobile or can't function to swim correctly. To combat male infertility, good nutrition can be vital—high in vitamins A, D, E, and K, as well as vitamin C (for increased production and mobility) and zinc (found in high concentrations in sperm). In addition, it is important to eat hormone-free animal products—organic meats and grass-fed meats. If a male's mother ate the wrong meats during pregnancy, such may also have had an impact on her son's fertility.

What to do if nothing seems to help, other than IVF? As said before, it needs to be stated first that duties and rights go together. As there is no duty to marry, so there is no right to marry. In a similar way, as there is no duty to have offspring, so there is no right to have offspring. The *Catechism* (2378) says, "A child is not something owed to one, but is a gift." And elsewhere (2378), "A child may not be considered a piece of property, an idea to which an alleged 'right to a child' would lead." Therefore, infertility is not something we have a moral duty to combat. Combatting infertility is a personal choice. Yet there may be many reasons for trying to do so.

In biblical times, the chief value of a woman was first her chastity and, after marriage, her reproductivity. The Bible has many examples of couples who were infertile—names such as Rachel, Sarah, and Elizabeth come to mind. Most of them were temporarily infertile. God used their infertility to show his miraculous power and to carry out his plan for human history. The most notable infertile woman in the Bible is Hannah (1 Samuel 2). Consumed by thoughts of her infertility, she went alone to the temple and cried her heart out to God. She made drastic promises to the Lord in hopes she would be given a child. She was stabbed with the pain of watching other women easily conceive and bear children. In Hannah, we see a truthful picture of the pain of infertility.

To those couples who went through similar experiences and had to finally give up their battle against infertility, the *Catechism* (2379) speaks with deep compassion: "The Gospel shows that physical sterility is not an absolute evil. Spouses who still suffer from infertility after exhausting legitimate medical procedures should unite themselves with the Lord's Cross, the source of all spiritual fecundity." Earlier we said that in a marriage love is first, and then comes procreation; it is from this love that the ardent desire of fruitfulness originates. When infertility prevents biological fruitfulness in a marriage, that fact in itself does not have to extinguish or diminish the love between wife and husband, and their fruitfulness. Instead, in the words of Alice von Hildebrand, "it might channel their fruitfulness in other directions, for example, by adopting orphans or abandoned children, or by having spiritual children." The *Catechism* (2379) speaks in similar terms about such couples: "They can give expression to their generosity by adopting abandoned children or performing demanding services for others." This may sound like a cold suggestion, but many couples have found real fulfillment of life in following this advice. It is a cross that may become a blessing for others.

5

Abortion

T he practice of abortion—the medical removal of an unborn baby from a woman's womb on her request—has always been a conflict of interests: the interests of the mother versus the interests of the child. It is a conflict that has been known since at least ancient times. In the interest of the mother, various methods were used to perform an abortion, including the administration of abortifacient herbs, the use of sharpened implements, the application of abdominal pressure, and other techniques. Such techniques were generally outlawed, and the Hippocratic Oath explicitly forbade the use of medical techniques to induce abortion, no matter what the woman's interests were.

A Conflict of Interests

Recently, we have seen a dramatic twist in the abortion debate. We discussed already how the so-called "sexual revolution," unleashed in the 1960s, had an enormous impact on human sexuality and "traditional" morality. As with most revolutions, the sexual revolution changed the meaning of words. Just as the French revolution changed even the names of streets and rivers, the sexual revolution attempted to create dramatic changes in the moral vocabulary of an entire society, detaching love from marriage, sex from marriage, sex from procreation, and procreation from marriage. The word "love" became another word for sex, and the word "sex" became identical to lust. George Orwell famously warned that when words are emptied of their original meanings, a host of demons will rush in to take up residence within their comfortable confines.

Hence there was no more role for morality left, at best a "morality" of so-called hedonism, which makes pleasure the one and only "good" thing in life. It could be called "secular hedonism," the worldview that sex is a sterile recreational activity, with babies thrown in as an optional afterthought for people with quirky lifestyle preferences. Hedonism is another example of the naturalistic fallacy: it defines something moral, "good," in terms of something natural, "pleasure." Thus it makes a quasi-moral claim that life "ought" to be as pleasurable, comfortable, and stimulating as we can make it, so that any unwanted consequences should be removed. Its slogan is, in essence, "it's all about pleasure"—the pleasure of food, drinks, drugs, and money, but most of all of sex. Hedonism is one of those "isms" that narrow everything down to one aspect of life—actually to one small part of the brain, the limbic system—while neglecting the truth that there is more to life, and to the brain.

Lost in the process is the Catholic view that love in a marriage is a reflection of God's love for us, so that sexuality in a marriage is a reflection of God's creative power—the creation of new life. Pope Francis, in his Apostolic Exhortation *The Joy of Love* (151) says, "Sexuality is not a means of gratification or entertainment; it is an interpersonal language wherein the other is taken seriously, in his or her sacred and inviolable dignity." The only thing that the sexual revolution has left us is lust—pleasure gone wild—which the *Catechism* (2351) calls "disordered desire for or inordinate enjoyment of sexual pleasure. Sexual pleasure is morally disordered when sought for itself, isolated from its procreative and unitive purposes." This made Peter Kreeft quip, "Freud thought love was a substitute for lust. Christ knew that lust was a substitute for love."

The ideas of the "Sexual Revolution" soon flooded the Western world. But it was especially a new technique, artificial contraception, that made it physically possible for almost any person to reduce sexuality to a mere recreational activity without any further life-changing consequences. From then on, sexual activity has become a morally neutral activity—as long as it is private and consensual. The new slogan is "What we do behind closed doors is nobody's business." And in case contraception fails, the unforeseen and unwanted "product" should be aborted, as "a nuisance that should not be."

The sexual revolution was meant to "liberate" men and women from any stifling morality. They were now supposedly "free" to follow their own interests instead of antiquated traditions and moral codes. It is a new freedom of "self-determination," making us believe that we are fully self-made, in full control of our own history and destination. Human freedom presumably means that one is able to choose and act according to the "dictates" of one's own will. The sexual revolution reduced those "dictates" to personal interests and personal desires in matters of sexuality—sex for recreational purposes, but certainly not for procreation. But history has shown us that Freud and his followers were wrong: complete sexual freedom has not made us psychologically healthier, quite the contrary—it has deeply sickened our society. Sexual freedom has turned out to be a false promise.

How different is the Catholic understanding of human freedom! Freedom is never unlimited. First of all, "freedom" stands for our *capacity* to make choices, because we have a free will. But even that capacity is not unlimited. Our freedom of self-determination does not let us do whatever we want to do. The more we are aware of the physical and psychological constraints that limit our freedom, the more we can actually be free. "Know yourself," says an old inscription in Delphi. With the proper knowledge of ourselves, we can take charge of our constraints so that we are no longer their victims, but rather their architects. That is our capacity for freedom.

But "freedom" is more than a capacity. It also stands for the moral *right* of freedom that all humans share. However, this freedom too is not unlimited. For instance, we cannot use the right of freedom to abolish the right of freedom. The right of free speech does not give us the right to utter any kind of speech, including hate speech. More importantly, the moral right of freedom is not under its own authority. Moral rights are God-given and are ultimately under God's authority. Some people reject this view because they erroneously believe that human beings lose their freedom when they live "under God."

The Church proclaims quite the opposite! Because "I" was made in God's image, "I" become more myself when I grow closer to God's likeness. Only those who are reconciled with God can also be reconciled with themselves and become more in harmony with themselves. But once creatures separate themselves from their Creator, they lose their identity. In other words, we have been given the freedom to choose, not whatever we *desire* to do, but what we *ought* to do in order to become more ourselves.

The sexual revolution sees abortion from a very different perspective, as simply a matter of conflicting *interests*. But then, in a cunning twist, it turns a woman's interest into a woman's right: the woman has the "moral right of freedom" to do with her own body whatever is in her own interest. But what about the baby's interest? When talking about interests, we have to face a conflict between the interests of a liberated woman and the interests of... Yes, of what? There are actually no interests on the other side of the conflict, according to this new understanding. To make sure pregnancy becomes a matter of a woman's interests *only*, the next step is to change the meaning of what it is that she is pregnant with. It is no longer a human being but mere "tissue," a "growth," a "tumor," a "clump of cells" foreign to the woman's body. Abortion supporters simply define the unborn out of existence. Once the unborn child has become a "nothing" and is no longer a separate individual, the entire focus of the conflict has been redirected to the mother only.

Obviously, "clumps of cells" cannot express any desires or defend any interests—they are voiceless. Since a growing clump of cells cannot have interests or desires, there is no longer a conflict of interests—all that is left are the woman's interests. We are supposed to adjust our terminology and vocabulary to that fact, for abortion is too harsh a word for the removal of a clump of cells without voice, without desires, without interests. From then on, abortion is something like the removal of an appendix. Some have even chosen to label abortion as a "cure" for the "disease" of pregnancy, thus turning abortion into a "health" issue; it is something decided on by the woman for her own well-being, and according to her own desires and interests. It makes for a pro-choice position. Since there are no interests on the other side of the conflict, there is not even a conflict left, and the woman is free to choose. The new mantra is, "It is *my* body, so I can decide whatever *I* want." From now on, the choice for abortion has become the key to social liberation, an objective and moral "good" that should never be apologized for.

The ultimate aim behind all of this is to erase the word "abortion" from our vocabulary entirely, so that the idea of a "conflict," let alone a moral dilemma, no longer exists. It is no longer an abortion, but a woman's "health" issue. Everything related to it, including abortive contraception, has become a "health care" issue too, in spite of the fact that none of this has anything to do with the health of the mother, let alone the health of her to-be-aborted unborn baby. Abortion can only be called a health care issue if pregnancy is considered a disease. It is shocking how pro-choice activists consistently avoid using the word "abortion." Instead they replace it with more neutral or better-sounding terminology. They call themselves "pro-choice" instead of "pro-abortion," and they vow to avoid the word "abortion" entirely. Words certainly matter!

Changing terminology is a sly way of hiding and suppressing any moral issues. A similar "trick" was once used during the 1964–65 rubella outbreak when children were born with the congenital rubella syndrome, which caused blindness and other medical complications. Abortion was recommended as a "therapeutic solution." Currently we see this happening again with pregnant women infected with the Zika virus, which may cause microcephaly. This makes the same advocates speak again of "therapeutic" solutions. The word "therapeutic" means "healing," but abortion does not heal anything; instead, it ends innocent lives. Ironically, those who see abortion as a good thing for women should be proud enough to use that word frequently, yet they prefer to hide it or disguise it. They prefer to describe their opponents not as "pro-life" but as "anti-choice."

This creates a much-skewed view of what is really going on. Peter Kreeft gives a good assessment of the current situation:

> The moral revolution is confined to sex. We are not allowed to steal another man's money without being put into jail, but we can steal another man's wife. You cannot betray your lawyer without being severely penalized, but you can betray your wife, and she is

severely penalized. You cannot kill bald eagles or blue whales without being a criminal but you can kill your own children as long as you do it a second before the two blades of the scissors meet in the middle of the umbilical cord rather than a second after, or a second before the body emerges from the birth canal rather than a second after. What kind of logic is this?

Sex is certainly a very powerful drive in life. If not curbed, it can have devastating effects. Peter Kreeft hit the nail on the head: "If storks brought babies, Planned Parenthood would go broke. Sex is the motor that drives the abortion business." The struggle to overcome abortion begins with the struggle to keep sex in its proper context, which requires discipline and self-mastery.

We all know and acknowledge that slavery or Nazism was a public evil a while ago, but what is the public evil of our time? Anthony Esolen doesn't hesitate to answer: the Sexual Revolution. He asks the question, "What is worse—to be a clerk in a Nazi train station or to be a clerk in a Planned Parenthood clinic?" True, the former was more risky then than the latter is now. But the question remains: Which one has caused more deaths? Those who take what they were brought up with for granted would probably vote for the former. But we cannot ignore the fact that the sexual revolution has also left a trail of death.

Because the sexual revolution identifies love with sex, sex has taken over. Sex addiction has become a devastating epidemic in our society. There are only two methods to stop the epidemic. Method number one is discipline and self-mastery. The *Catechism* (2339) describes self-control, also called self-mastery, as "a training in human freedom" and goes on as follows, "The alternative is clear: either man governs his passions and finds peace, or he lets himself be dominated by them and becomes unhappy." We need to become masters of our feelings and emotions, not their slaves. The one word for sexual virtue is chastity. Chastity does not mean abstinence of sexual intercourse, although it may include it. It means purity: pure sex, right sex, not twisted sex. Since we are often tempted to kinky sex, chastity requires self-control, self-mastery. Not only should we learn to say No to taking drugs, but also No to having sex out of lust.

Method number two for stopping the epidemic of sex addiction is that of placing sexuality back where it belongs: within the sanctity of marriage. Peter Kreeft minces no words, "We moderns think sex is for us; it isn't; it's for our children." And "the most essential thing about sex, the essential meaning and purpose of sex, the very essence of sex is this: Sex creates babies. They're not accidents! Pregnancy is not a disease." Although there is more to sexuality than creating babies, it is in a woman's body that God re-enters the world as Creator. Abortion, on the other hand, is, in Kreeft's words, "backup birth control, and birth control is the demand to have sex without having babies. If the stork brought babies, there'd be no Planned Parenthood."

Returning to our original question, do a woman and a newborn have conflicting interests in the abortion debate? Of course they do: the interests of the unborn having the desire to live versus the interests of the mother having the desire for free choice. The "drive" to live is anchored in nature; even animals will fight for it to their very last breath. Of course, one can object that animals would not exist anymore if they did not have this drive. But such an argument only questions how that drive came along, not whether it exists. It exists also, or even more so, in human beings, who derive their human dignity from the fact that they are made in God's image—they want to live, they have the right to live, and they have the duty to live. Other human beings have the duty to respect that right. This makes it very hard to claim that abortion is basically the same as an appendix operation.

Contrary to popular opinion, abortion hurts women. The *Medical Science Monitor* published alarming data in 2003 and 2004. Here are some results. Women have a 65% higher risk of clinical depression following abortion compared to childbirth. Abortion increases a woman's risk of future miscarriages by 60%. Suicide rates among women who have abortions are six times higher than those who give birth. Their death rates from various causes after abortion are 3.5 times higher than after giving birth. We should conclude that abortion is more of a "nightmare" than a "healthy choice." Some 60% of women surveyed after abortion responded, "Part of me died." This doesn't quite sound like the removal of an appendix.

A Conflict of Rights

Not only can there be a conflict of personal *interests* between the mother and the unborn baby, but, more importantly, there is also the possibility of a conflict of moral *rights*. Whereas interests are about subjective personal feelings and desires, rights are about objective moral duties and responsibilities. Interests are a matter of likes and dislikes, but rights are about do's and do-not-do's.

What "rights" are we talking about here? No one can have a right to something unless it belongs to him or her in some way. No one has a right to something from the mere fact that he or she wants it, or that somebody else would like them to have it—those are mere personal interests, perhaps entitlements, but not absolute rights. What belongs to a human being is the right to life. Therefore, the unborn has the right to life as much as the mother has this right—this is a God-given right, and no one should ever take it away.

We discussed earlier the fact that the unborn, from conception on, is a human being, and with its humanity comes the right to be given *human dignity*—a moral right that everyone has the duty to respect. The *Catechism* (2274) says, "Since it must be treated from conception as a person, the embryo must be defended in its integrity, cared for, and healed, as far as possible, like any other human being." The Bible tells us, "Before I formed you in the womb I knew you, and before you were born I consecrated you" (Jer. 1:5). Therefore, abortion is always wrong, for there are no biological criteria that would make it morally right. As said earlier, one cannot use relative biological standards of viability, maturity, health, fitness, and the like to measure or judge the absolute moral value of human life, its human dignity, and its human rights. Rights are God-given rights, not man-made entitlements.

The most basic principle of the Christian moral life is the proclamation that every person bears the dignity of being made in the image of God, from the moment of conception on. Unfortunately, the moral concept of human dignity has been misinterpreted many times. When the United Nations in its 1948 *Universal Declaration of Human Rights* assumed a generally shared understanding of "human dignity," going back to its Judeo-Christian roots, it failed to define it in order to achieve passage. As a result, the declaration of human rights was put at the mercy of special-interest groups who came up with new "rights," practically invented on the spot.

Soon, new sexual and reproductive "rights," such as abortion, were included, and so were the new "rights" of scientists to experiment with human embryos, as well as another invention, the "last civil right" to die. Although "pro-choice" activists do not take rights as absolute, let alone God-given, they happily take on the terminology of "rights." They speak of "pro-choice rights" to defend them against the claims of "pro-life rights." Or they set the "rights" of LGBT people against the "beliefs" of certain religious groups. But that is exactly where the problem lies. If one group has "rights," then the other group must have them too. If one group has only "beliefs," then the other group must have beliefs too.

Obviously, the concept of human dignity had become what Adam Schulman called "a placeholder for whatever it is about human beings that entitles them to basic human rights and freedoms." It became an issue of "political correctness"—an elastic concept that can be redefined anytime according to anyone's wishes. That is how abortion was renamed as a "reproductive right," in spite of the fact that this makes for a strange interpretation. How could a "reproductive right" ever allow for abortion *after* the reproduction has already taken place? True, women are free to make reproductive choices *before* they get pregnant, but not after, for then it is too late. The moment we start to call abortion and abortive contraceptives "health care" issues—or anything else that they are not—we find ourselves in a terminological jumble, for none of this has anything to do with the health of the mother, let alone the health of the to-be-aborted unborn baby.

Yet organizations such as Planned Parenthood follow this strategy of redefining core terminology very closely, cloaking their activities and procedures in euphemisms—clinical descriptions of what is actually going on. Yearly, they perform some 330,000 abortions in the USA, but they don't describe them that way. They speak of "dilation and evacuation" when a fetus is torn apart and then drawn out of the uterus. They speak of "dilation and extraction" when a doctor delivers a baby except for the head, and then punches a hole in the back of the head to suck out the brain, ensuring that the baby is not born alive. And recently we found out that they even harvest parts of aborted babies for commercial purposes under the pretext of organ "donations." But euphemisms do not change the fact that abortion is killing. Asked to name the single most important of his many social principles of reform, the legendary Chinese philosopher Confucius answered, "The restoration of language," that is, calling things by their proper names. The question is not "Who decides?" but "Who dies?"

Abortion activists have often protested that a woman has the right to human freedom as much as anyone else, so she has the right to choose for or against abortion—it is *her* body, and therefore *her* choice. They further argue that gender equality would be advanced if women could be as liberated from the prospects of pregnancy as men are. Do they not have a point here? Is not human freedom an inalienable right? As a matter of fact, the Catholic Church herself praises the right of human freedom. The *Catechism* (1738) says it clearly:

> Freedom is exercised in relationships between human beings. Every human person, created in the image of God, has the natural right to be recognized as a free and responsible being. All owe to each other this duty of respect. The right to the exercise of freedom, especially in moral and religious matters, is an inalienable requirement of the dignity of the human person.

However, human freedom is more than a *capacity* to choose between this and that. In the words of the *Catechism* (1740), "The exercise of freedom does not imply a right to say or do everything." Ultimately, human freedom is under a higher authority and subject to moral standards: some choices are morally good, others are morally bad or evil. In contrast, many people today understand human freedom merely as the ability to make a choice, with no objective norm or good as the goal: "Do as you like." Interestingly enough, pro-choice activists are highly selective in their pro-choice positions. They are pro-choice as long as your choice matches theirs. They are pro-choice in choosing abortion, but they are usually not pro-choice in matters of gun control, the death penalty, free speech, or slavery.

Besides, if a woman claims her free choice *after* becoming pregnant, she should first of all claim her free choice *before* becoming pregnant.

Yes, we do have a free choice when it comes to morality, but that does not mean we can choose whatever we want. We cannot vote to decide whether we are anti-slavery and anti-abortion, or not. Slavery, which seems to be such a clear case, was legal in the United States a short time ago. Law professor Robert George likes to ask his college students how many of them, if they lived in the South before the Civil War, would have opposed slavery. They all raise their hands. "Bless their hearts," says he, and tells them what their opposition would have cost them: ridicule, slander, or much worse. It is easy to take a relativistic stance. Had the slaveholders won the Civil War, we might today view slavery as an admirable institution.

Let us apply this attitude to more recent times. Had we lived in Nazi Germany, we would all be an Oskar Schindler or a Corrie ten Boom; we would never have caught the nationalist and socialist disease. Really? It is hard to believe, since this requires, as Anthony Esolen describes it, "Self-surgery without anesthesia: to tear some feature of your errant culture out of your flesh. [...] You have to embrace an authority over against what everybody knows, what everybody says, what everybody does; and this authority must do more than recommend. It must command, even in the face of suffering, doubt, and failure." In other words, we are under a higher Authority, in spite of the fact that many claim nowadays that there is no higher authority than "Me, Myself, and I." That is exactly how Eve was tempted in Paradise, "You will be like God, knowing good and evil" (Gen. 3:5).

In this context, Pope John Paul II has drawn attention to the two radically different meanings of the word "my." When I say, "This is my cell phone," I mean that I *own* the phone. On the other hand, when I say, "This is my wife," it is clear that I am not claiming that I own her, but that I am *part* of her. So what do we say when a pregnant woman says "It's *my* body, therefore I can do with it whatever I want, including an abortion"? In a sense, it is indeed her body, something she owns, for she can control the use of her arm, for instance, by choosing to swing her arm. But as we said earlier, we do not *have* a body, we *are* a body. In that particular sense, our body is not a machine that we own. It is "my" body but not "mine." If there is anyone who owns my body, it is the one who made it, God. Therefore, I cannot sell or kill my own body. In a similar way, a pregnant woman cannot do whatever she wants with her body. Even if she is in control of what she does with her body, such control must also include moral control.

Even if a woman were allowed to do with her body whatever she wants, we need to admit that the unborn baby is not *her* body. The baby is *in* her body, yes, but it is not a *part* of her body—it is a genetically distinct being. Therefore, abortion does not only affect her own body, but also someone else's body, that of the unborn baby. Why would a pregnant woman not allow the baby a right to his or her own body, when she claims this right so insistently for herself? Does the unborn baby not have the same right to say: "This is my body, and not yours!" Pope Francis says in *The Joy of Love* (170): "A child is a human being of immense worth and may never be used for one's own benefit. So it matters little whether this new life is convenient for you, whether it has features that please you, or whether it fits into your plans and aspirations."

The new person in a mother's womb is not a part of her body, but someone who has his or her own little body. It is another person that she is now "part" of and responsible for. Parents are not owners of their children, born or unborn, but rather their guardians or stewards. The *Catechism* (2378) confirms this: "A child is not something owed to one, but is a gift. The 'supreme gift of marriage' is a human person. A child may not be considered a piece of property, an idea to which an alleged 'right to a child' would lead." This certainly puts the slogan of pro-choice women, "It is *my* body," in an entirely different perspective.

In other words, morality is not about the choices we have, but about the choices that are morally right; it obliges us to go for pro-life and pro-abolition, otherwise we would make a moral mistake. Pro-choice, on the other hand, is a statement under a moral disguise that allows one to disregard human rights. But one cannot use morality to abolish morality by claiming one particular "right" that would allow us to abolish all moral rights. That would be comparable to Hitler using democracy to abolish democracy. A pro-choice position is at best a matter of interests, never a matter of rights. No woman has the right to deny her unborn baby the right to life. It may be inconvenient to her to continue her pregnancy, but it is never morally right to terminate her pregnancy (except in "crisis" situations; see below). A child is a "gift," not a "choice."

Many are so "blind" to this absolute moral value of human life and its sanctity that they need an ultrasound to "see," with their own eyes, the evidence of what is morally wrong with abortion. Moral blindness has been spreading on its way to a majority vote. In history, how often were the best people, who had the clearest discernment of moral values, persecuted by the blind majority! And yet, the advancement of humanity often depended on these very people, who had a sharper and better discernment of moral values. As we are grateful for the anti-slavery activists of the past, perhaps someday, most of us will also be grateful to the anti-abortion activists, including the unwavering moral voice of the Church. In other words, it is not moral values that change, but our moral evaluations—that is, our subjective attitudes toward these objective and universal values.

Fortunately, there are also modern technologies that have helped us to cure moral blindness. As mentioned earlier, the use of ultrasounds allows us to "see" inside the uterus, making a pregnant mother more aware of what—or rather who—is growing in the hidden recesses of her womb. There are currently 29 states that demand ultrasounds prior to abortions. It was this technology that changed Dr. Bernard Nathanson from pro-choice to pro-life as far back in 1979, when the first generation of ultrasounds convinced this man— a self-described "Jewish atheist" who was one of America's leading abortionists and co-founder of what is now NARAL Pro-Choice America—that he was killing unborn children.

Some have managed to come up with another false set of rights— so-called "animal rights." Such people value the lives of baby animals, such as seals, more than the lives of unborn babies. Simple common sense tells us that animals have no moral rights. As we said earlier, animals never do awful things out of meanness or cruelty, for the simple reason that they have no morality. Therefore, they have no duties and responsibilities, and consequently no rights. If animals had moral rights, their fellow animals would have the moral duty to respect those rights as well. If animals had moral rights, we should hold them accountable for their actions.

Since Charles Darwin, we have been brainwashed into degrading human beings to the status of glorified animals, or vice versa— inflating animals to pre-humans. Darwin and his followers only look at our biology and miss out on the spiritual dimension of humanity which comes with rationality and morality. Even if they do acknowledge rationality and morality, they still reduce them to mere biology. Our inability to let animals be animals has something to do with our inability to let human beings be human beings.

Human dignity is probably the most central, but also the most challenging, concept in Catholic morality. It applies to everyone, born or unborn, healthy or disabled, rich or poor, attractive or repulsive, friend or enemy. It is very hard, if not impossible, to live this command to the fullest, for we "naturally" tend to make a difference between the former and the latter. We repeatedly and constantly sin against the fact that we are all children of the same Father, who has no favorites. Only a few Saints lived up to that truth. St. Damien, for instance, spent most of his life restoring the human dignity of the lepers at Molokai in Hawaii; although often overwhelmed by the stench of their rotting flesh, daily he touched, hugged, and bathed them. St. Peter Claver took care of the slaves that arrived by the thousands every year in Cartagena, the center of the slave trade in South America; he even showed affection to afflicted slaves by kissing their open wounds. One needs to be a Saint to go this far, yet we are all called to at least strive for sainthood. That is how pivotal the right and duty of human dignity is for each one of us; it stretches as far as the fight for the human dignity of the smallest and most defenseless of us all, the unborn.

The reader may remember a billboard in Manhattan which read as follows: *The most dangerous place for an African-American is in the womb.* Some may defuse this as a racist remark, but it is actually racial love speech, not racial hate speech; in 2013 black women accounted for 29,007 terminated pregnancies, representing almost 42 percent of all abortions in the city. That same year, black women in the city gave birth to 24,108 babies. With abortions surpassing live births by nearly 5,000, African-American women in the city clearly terminated pregnancies more often than they carried babies to term. Black women terminated pregnancies at a rate of 67.3 per 1,000 women ages 15 to 49, a rate far higher than any other racial or ethnic group. Dr. Elveda King, Martin Luther's King niece, calls abortion "the civil rights issue of our times." It is a matter of fact that the womb is the most dangerous place for African-Americans in New York City. We should ask them, and ourselves: Is there any sanctuary left if even the womb of a pregnant mother is no longer a safe hiding place for new life? The controversy over abortion is not a matter of beliefs or opinions, but a matter of life or death.

Crisis Situations

The Catholic Church has always defended the sanctity of human life. Not only is this stand thoroughly biblical, but it is also found in the Didache (c. AD 80), the oldest source of ecclesiastical law and, after the New Testament, the first Christian catechism. The pertinent passage reads, "You shall not slay the child by abortion." Nonetheless, many non-Catholics, but also some Catholics, accuse the Catholic Church of an inconsistent morality when it comes to killing. Killing in the womb is forbidden, they say, but killing in self-defense or in war or through the death penalty is accepted. These people ask for what they call a more "consistent ethic of life." Do they have a point?

The Catholic Church actually has a rather nuanced view on this issue. First of all, she makes a distinction between killing and murder, which can be found in the Bible. "You shall not kill" is not a command found in the Ten Commandments; in its original language, the command from Scripture reads, "You shall not murder" (Exodus 20:13). The Hebrew word for "murder" literally means "the intentional, premeditated killing of another person with malice." Killing becomes murder when (and only when) it is not properly justified, and the justifications are clear: You may use whatever force necessary to protect your own life from a hostile aggressor, or to save the life of an innocent person from such imminent, life-threatening danger. But never can one of the Ten Commandments be pitted against another—there simply is no conflict among the Commandments. Respect for life does not mean that one can, should, or must break one of the other Commandments.

There are many situations in which killing is not murder, especially in cases of self-defense or defense of others. The *Catechism* (2264) confirms this: "Someone who defends his life is not guilty of murder even if he is forced to deal his aggressor a lethal blow." And elsewhere (2265): "Legitimate defense can be not only a right but a grave duty for one who is responsible for the lives of others." This could even be applied to the Church's social teaching regarding a "just war" as a means to defend life and property or to recover lost territory. It assumes that killing enemies is indeed evil, but also acknowledges that remaining passive in the face of violence might be a greater evil. It might be better to speak of a "just peace" instead—not as a form of pacifism, but as a means to prevent or limit war rather than to endorse war.

Something similar may be said about capital punishment. The continuous teaching of the Church has always been, not only that capital punishment is in principle legitimate, but also that it is in principle legitimate precisely as a means of securing retributive justice. Cardinal Avery Dulles put it this way:

> The real issue for Catholics is to determine the circumstances under which that penalty ought to be applied. [...] The doctrine remains what it has been: that the State, in principle, has the right to impose the death penalty on persons convicted of very serious crimes. But the classical tradition held that the State should not exercise this right when the evil effects outweigh the good effects. Thus the principle still leaves open the question whether and when the death penalty ought to be applied.

The Church defends her position by using Aquinas's Principle of Double Effect. In the words of the *Catechism* (2263): "The act of self-defense can have a double effect: the preservation of one's own life; and the killing of the aggressor.... The one is intended, the other is not." This principle relies on the distinction between a good effect that one intends and an evil effect that one does not intend. According to this principle, it may be morally permissible to perform an act with double effect, but only if all of the following criteria are fulfilled: (1) the act is not morally wrong; (2) the good effect is directly intended; (3) the bad effect is only indirectly intended; (4) the bad effect is not the means for attaining the good effect; and (5) the good effect outweighs the bad effect. Therefore, self-defense is morally justified: one may use violence against another to save one's own life, even if a consequence of self-defense will be the death of the aggressor.

Because of this principle, killing does not always equate to murder. This made Cardinal Ratzinger, the later Pope Benedict XVI, say: "While the Church exhorts civil authorities to seek peace, not war, and to exercise discretion and mercy in imposing punishment on criminals, it may still be permissible to take up arms to repel an aggressor or to have recourse to capital punishment." This statement could easily be seen as an answer to the call for a "consistent ethic of life," for there is nothing inconsistent about this view.

The question now is, of course, whether this position also holds for the abortion debate. Does it follow that abortion can be lethal without being murder? Could there be situations in which abortion would be the best solution of several worse alternatives? A first response would be: There are no gradations in good and evil; there is no "lesser evil" or "greater good." New wrongs cannot erase previous wrongs, but can only add to them by making things worse. Evil is evil, no matter how you look at it. "A greater good" can never permit "minor evils," for how could good ever originate from evil? In morality, there is no "greater" versus "lesser," because morality is not about relative criteria, but about absolute standards. The good of saving a mother's life can never offset the evil of killing a human life through abortion.

Yet, there may be circumstances in which the Principle of Double Effect kicks in: a good effect one intends and an evil effect one does *not* intend. Could this apply even to abortion? Let us state first that medical considerations can never overrule moral considerations. Medical rules should always comply with the moral rule of preserving life, for morality is not a calculus of consequences, depending on circumstances or the end in view. Abortion may sometimes be medically right, but that does not automatically make it also morally right. Every obstetrician should always take care of *two* patients—

both the mother and her unborn baby. However, there may be medical reasons for abortion—such as the life of the pregnant mother being in danger—and those reasons need to be taken into moral consideration.

Second, it should be stressed that the medical situation of the mother should never be put against the medical situation of the unborn baby. In trying to find exceptions to the abortion prohibition in the interest of providing better care for the pregnant woman, the Church never treated one form of human life as more important than another. Pope Pius XII made this point very clear when he stated: "Never and in no case has the Church taught that the life of the child must be preferred to that of the mother. It is erroneous to put the question with this alternative: either the life of the child or that of the mother."

In this context, the Canadian philosopher Donald DeMarco mentions how Thomas Aquinas dealt with a similar question—whether it is permissible to section the uterus of a pregnant woman if this is the only way to baptize the fetus that is in danger of dying. Aquinas refuses to allow this and quotes St. Paul, who says in Rom. 3:8, "We should not do evil that there may come good." Aquinas considered it an impermissible evil to impose direct physical harm on a pregnant woman (in all probability causing her death) with the good intention of baptizing her unborn baby in order to save the unborn for eternal salvation. This would make one form of human life more important than another. On the other hand, it would be morally permissible to remove the fallopian tube in case of an ectopic pregnancy, or to remove a cancerous uterus, since the primary purpose of these therapeutic procedures is to save the life of the mother, not to destroy the fetus—a consequence that happens indirectly or accidentally.

Let us analyze the Principle of Double Effect a bit further for cases in which a woman has a rather serious pathological condition during her pregnancy. Operations, treatments, and medications that will result in the death of the unborn baby may be morally permissible if—and only if—their direct purpose is to cure the pregnant woman, and if they cannot be safely postponed until the unborn baby is viable. In other words, actions that may result in the death of an unborn baby *might* be morally permitted, but only if all of the following conditions are met: (1) treatment is directly therapeutic in response to a serious pathology of the mother or child; (2) the good effect of curing the disease is intended; (3) the bad effect is foreseen but not intended; (4) the death of the unborn baby is not the means by which the good effect is achieved; (5) the good of curing the disease is proportionate to the risk of the bad effect.

The Principle of Double Effect is an important directive in crisis situations when there is a conflict of two lives being in danger. It allows for killing of the unborn which is not murder. On the other hand, the killing of the unborn is certainly not mandatory in cases like these. Famous is the case of St. Gianna Beretta Molla, an Italian pediatrician who was also a wife and a mother; she died on April 28, 1962. During the second month of her fourth pregnancy, she developed a fibroma on her uterus. After examining her, the doctors gave her three choices: an abortion, a complete hysterectomy, or removal of only the fibroma. Molla refused both an abortion and a hysterectomy, despite knowing that continuing with the pregnancy could result in her own death, as it in fact did.

The Principle of Double Effect would have allowed Molla to undergo a hysterectomy, which might have caused her unborn child's death as an unintended consequence. Instead, she opted for the removal of the fibroma, wanting to preserve her child's life. She unselfishly deemed her baby's life more important than her own. On April 21, 1962, Molla went to the hospital, where her fourth child, Gianna Emanuela, was successfully delivered by Caesarean section. However, Molla continued to have severe pain, and died of septic peritonitis seven days after giving birth. Gianna Emanuela lives today and is a doctor of geriatrics.

Pro-choice advocates have said that Molla's canonization suggests that the Catholic Church values an unborn child over the safety of a woman. Nothing is farther from the truth. Vatican officials immediately replied that although the Church admires women who sacrifice themselves to save a fetus, it does not oblige anyone to make this choice. Sacrificing oneself is neither a moral right nor a moral duty. It is an act of love done after the example of Jesus, who sacrificed his own life for our salvation.

6

Eugenics

Eugenics is a controversial set of beliefs and practices aimed at improving the genetic quality of the human population. There is a "negative" form of eugenics, aimed at preventing genetic diseases, and a "positive" form aimed at actively promoting favored genetic features. The prefix "eu-" in eugenics means "good" and gives the word a quasi-moral qualification, but eugenics is certainly not always "good." Eugenics calls for a moral assessment. Let us begin with "negative eugenics."

Negative Eugenics

Hardly anyone would deny that parents have a moral responsibility for their children, not only for their mental wellbeing, but also for their physical wellbeing. All of us have the right to lead a "good" life, but that also entails the duty of giving a "good" life to the next generation. As the *Catechism* (2288) puts it, "Life and physical health are precious gifts entrusted to us by God. We must take reasonable care of them, taking into account the needs of others and the common good." From a moral point of view, the parental role is one of altruistic commitment to the welfare of the child. People who want to be parents should want to be parents in order to give, not to get. Considering the welfare of the child means also considering the physical wellbeing of the child—including the kind and quality of life a child will have if affected by a genetic disorder. This could create a serious moral dilemma: What to do when you know you have a serious *genetic* disease? Do you want to pass this on to your children? And how serious is "serious"?

In an address to the participants of a medical symposium in 1953,

Pope Pius XII rejected the idea that individuals with undesirable genetic traits may be forbidden to marry and to bear children. But he also asked such individuals to consider the burden such a decision might impose on themselves, their spouse, and their offspring—a burden which might become intolerable. The Catholic Church gives a couple at risk for having a child with a genetic disorder two reproductive options to consider: either to take a chance and conceive naturally, with the intent of accepting the child whatever his or her condition, or to forgo having biological children, and either remain childless or adopt the children of others. If they decide to remain childless, they have to make another decision as to how to prevent procreation.

First, parents need to find out whether and which genetic disease they have. Of course, they already know if they have any easily detectable genetic diseases, such as epilepsy, blindness, or cystic fibrosis. But they may not know if they are a "carrier" of a recessive, hidden allele for a certain disease. To find out more, they might be well advised to go for genetic counseling (not to be confused with "genome testing," which provides information about one's ancestry for curious minds). Not only may genetic counseling inform them which diseases they may have or carry, but it will also tell them what the chances are that this genetic trait will be passed on to the next generation. Genetic counselors, if ethical, generally adopt a nondirective approach to working with clients. They give their clients relevant medical information and describe the options available, but will not tell clients which course of action to take.

What knowledge is their advice based on? In general, alleles for a certain disease are either recessive (let's use the notation a) or dominant (notation A). The carrier of a recessive allele (Aa) has a 50% chance to give the recessive allele to the next generation, but even then, it will remain recessive and hidden, unless his or her spouse is also a carrier of this allele (Aa). In the latter case, there is a 25% chance of giving birth to an affected child (aa). This is usually the case for genetic disorders such as cystic fibrosis, sickle-cell anemia, phenylketonuria, dwarfism, and albinism. For dominant alleles, the situation is different, as there are no carriers of hidden alleles. People with the disease may be either AA, with a 100% chance their child will have the disease too, or *Aa*, with a 50% chance of trans-mitting the disease. Examples are Huntington's chorea, Marfan's syndrome, and most forms of congenital deafness.

The situation is a bit more complicated when the allele is located on the X-chromosome. Well-known examples of this kind of inher-itance include certain forms of muscular dystrophy, hemophilia A and B, and red-green color blindness. Usually, such cases are reces-sive, which means that females possessing one X-linked recessive allele are considered carriers and will generally not manifest clinical symptoms of the disorder. On the other hand, all males possessing an X-linked recessive allele will be affected, because there is no sec-ond X-chromosome to compensate for this allele. All children of a female carrier have a 50% chance of inheriting the mutation. In males (*XY*), one allele is sufficient to cause the condition; in females *(XX)*, two alleles are needed to cause the disorder. All female chil-dren of an affected father will be carriers, for all daughters possess their father's X-chromosome. No male children of an affected father will be affected, as sons do not inherit their father's X-chromosome.

Unfortunately, the situation is more complicated than described here. Not too many diseases are based on either recessive or domi-nant alleles; there are many cases in-between, and there may be more variations of the allele. Also, the effect of such alleles often depends on the presence of alleles of other genes. Furthermore, the outcome can sometimes be prevented by lifestyle changes and diets (e.g., phenylketonuria)—another reason why genetic counseling is highly recommended. Based on this information, a couple should also find out which therapies are available for their potentially-affected baby after birth, which resources their family has available to enhance the condition of the child, and which social resources are available to help them do so. They should also find out how serious a "serious" disease is by talking to people who have that disease in their family. Whether to conceive is still is not an easy decision for a couple armed with such information to make, but no one else can make these decisions for them.

Couples should also should keep in mind that the importance of any genetic information they receive should not be overestimated; there is more to life than genetics. First of all, we do not really know whether one allele is "better" than another allele, since much depends on the surrounding genes and what impact they might have. Second, there are many diseases genetic counseling cannot foresee—various forms of cancer, allergies, Alzheimer's disease, and many, many more. Third, most people are healthy walking mutants, carrying all sorts of subtle and even rare genetic predispositions to disease. Everybody has genetic flaws; if you are looking for something wrong, you certainly will find it. The real issue is whether we need that genetic information, and if so, what to do with it. We should not forget that we all pass on genetic flaws to the next generation. Since we all die, all of us actually pass on a fatal disorder to our children—Original Sin.

Besides, even if things have gone "wrong" in a genetic or biological way, genetic disease does not make one a "failure." To use an analogy, when things go "wrong" in someone's life, career, or marriage, that does not mean that this person is a "lost case" who no longer deserves to live in our society. Genes are simply the hand that we are dealt; just as we may lose with a hand of "good" cards, we may be able to win with a "bad" hand. When problems loom, so do opportunities. As the legendary Congressman William Jennings Bryan used to say at the turn of the previous century, "Destiny is not a matter of chance; it is a matter of choice."

Another consideration is that there are always two people involved in procreation. The following anecdote shows this with some wit. When George Bernard Shaw was approached by a seductive young actress who cooed in his ear, "Wouldn't it be wonderful if we got married and had a child with my beauty and your brains?" Shaw replied, "My dear, that would be wonderful indeed, but what if our child had my beauty and your brains?" What this anecdote makes clear is that there is no procreation without "chances" or "risks." The outcome may be better than expected or worse than foreseen.

Finally, we should keep in mind that there are many other perspectives on human life apart from a genetic perspective, one of which is that humans live in a world of "good" and "evil." When we speak of "evil," we are asserting that evil "should" not exist. We are, in fact, evaluating a physical or genetic affliction as wrong or bad—

something no animal would be able to do. A prey animal does not consider its predator "evil"—perhaps painful, but not evil. When giving birth, animals may experience physical pain, but not suffering in the sense of something "bad" or "evil." Only humans take diseases, afflictions, and hardships as something that should not be, as something that seems to be acting against them personally. Animals may "dislike" these things, but they do not question them in terms of "Why *me?*" because they do not have a "me." Since animals do not know about good and bad, they cannot ask why bad things happen to good animals. Humans, on the other hand, know what the world "should" be like. We know of "evil" because we have an idea of what things would be like if everything were "good"—the way God intended them to be.

This forces us to look beyond genetics. Is a child with a genetic disorder less of a child? Of course not. Children are always a great good—a gift from God—whether or not they have been born with a disease. Who is going to decide which newly-discovered mutation goes on the list of "unwanted" alleles? Who will decide whether and when negative eugenics is called for? Most decisions concerning congenital mutations that condemn human beings—born or unborn—to destruction are arbitrarily made behind the closed doors of hospitals and pharmaceutical companies. Who gives anyone the right to make such decisions? As we mentioned earlier, everybody has genetic flaws and is, in essence, a walking genetic "junkyard"—including those who try to decide for us what is "unwanted."

In short, preventing what is "genetically flawed" is not a matter of genetics alone. Genetics can describe, but not prescribe; it cannot dictate morality. Many of those who have a handicap or disability are able to live a happy and healthy life despite the genetic challenge. To question this tells people living with disabilities that they are not worthy of existing and that their lives should not have been.

Ask people with mental or physical disabilities whether they feel worthless. If they say that they do, it is most likely that other people made them feel that way. People who have worked with children who have severe "defects," such as cerebral palsy, tell us that we should not get so absorbed in a "defect" that the normal development of the child becomes neglected. Only when caregivers focus on the normal part of the child's life can the child be properly challenged and grow to live a full life.

Having considered all of the above, couples who may pass on a serious genetic disease must make a decision either to forgo procreation or to take a "risk." If they choose to take the risk, do they still have the option to reverse their decision during pregnancy? Some believe that they should be able to do so, taking advantage of genetic tools currently available to test for such diseases during pregnancy—these methods are called "genetic testing" (not to be confused with genetic screening of the parents, which we mentioned earlier). Do they have a case?

Genetic testing is developing at rocket pace in our society. Its most common form is that of *prenatal* genetic testing—that is, testing the fetus during pregnancy. Since the 1980s, doctors have extracted samples of the embryo's outer membrane (chorionic villus sampling, or CVS) and of the fluid inside the inner membrane (amniocentesis) to diagnose genetic diseases such as Tay-Sachs syndrome and Down syndrome before the baby is born. It sounds promising and attractive, but is it? Genetic testing may seem a neutral activity, but its outcome may have dramatic consequences.

First, a word of medical caution. Because both aforementioned tests invade the womb for samples of fetal genetic material, they carry risks of infection and miscarriage. There is also a small risk that an amniocentesis could cause injury to the baby or mother, including an infection or preterm labor. Amniocentesis can even cause the birth defect of clubbed feet.

Second, a word of theoretical caution. Even though some genetic diseases, especially the ones based on a dominant allele, sound predetermined and inescapable, they are not a sure thing. Even if geneticists know that everyone with the disease carries one particular allele, they most likely do not know whether there are people walking around with that same allele who never developed the disease. The designation "dominant" versus "recessive" for an allele should always be a very cautious one.

Third, a word of philosophical caution. As said earlier, we should not forget that there is no "perfect" genome. If we did not want less-than-perfect children, no child would make the cut. Every day, researchers around the world report new disease-associated mutations in medical journals. Recent research suggests that every individual carries, on average, 313 disease-causing mutations. However, not all mutations cause disease. In any case, disease is a part of life; there is no human life without imperfection, nor one without suffering.

Finally, a word of moral caution. Recently, several firms began offering non-invasive blood tests for genetic disorders, such as Down syndrome, in which there are three instead of two copies of a particular chromosome. Additional non-invasive tests have been developed that promise to scan the whole genome of the fetus for more than 3,000 single-gene disorders. Such tests will almost certainly expand the "genetic grounds" for abortion—nicely, but deceivingly, dubbed "therapeutic abortion." As a matter of fact, most children diagnosed with Down syndrome in the womb never experience a birthday. Three different studies have estimated abortion rates for Down syndrome after genetic testing at 87%, 95%, and 98%.

One of the causes of these high numbers is that the prenatal diagnosis of Down syndrome is often accompanied by negative information, followed by the suggestion to terminate the pregnancy. Recently, a national law (2008) and three state laws—in Virginia (2007), Missouri (2011), and Massachusetts (2012)—mandated that women receive up-to-date and scientific information on paper from their health care providers, and that these providers recommend a referral to support groups or support services providers. Apparently, that was a much-needed mandate.

Unquestionably, we are being bombarded with a lot of misinformation on Down syndrome children in particular, referring to them with dehumanizing labels. Although it is true that children with Down syndrome used to be raised in institutions, today they are mostly brought home. As a result, many of them drive, work, marry, and even hold college degrees. Their life expectancy has quintupled, increasing from 12 years in 1912 to 60 years in 2012. People who know them say that there is something joyful, magnetic, and exuberant about them—even something therapeutic. Something similar could be said about many other people with genetic diseases.

Although genetic testing has led, and will lead, to more abortions on demand, we should also mention that genetic testing can be a positive and useful tool to better prepare parents for their special-needs children. Unfortunately, there is also another, darker side to genetic testing. It is almost inevitable that test results may be incorrect—so-called false positives. Incorrect test results may not only bring about wrong decisions, but will also lead to costly court rulings, which, in turn, will force companies to be mindful of the potential cost associated with any disability that arises if it could have been tested for prior to birth. Eventually, this may lead to forced pre-natal testing and forced abortion of babies with disabilities. We might be entering the doom-scenario announced in Aldous Huxley's *Brave New World*—negative eugenics at its worst.

The key question remains: Who decides if a newly-discovered mutation goes on the eugenicists' list of unwanted diseases? Defenders of negative eugenics cleverly swap one moral value, the sanctity of life, with another moral value, the prevention of suffering. They make it their "sacred mission" to prevent suffering at all cost, including the cost of unborn human life. Since words are inherently pliable, they can easily be adapted to any ideology. Some of these ideologists have put a nice label on this kind of abortion by calling it "eugenic abortion," but the concealed truth is that it eliminates everyone they deem not worth living. Supporters of eugenic abortion shift parental responsibility to governmental responsibility.

Positive Eugenics

The adjective "positive" in positive eugenics is an unfortunate choice, for it is far from positive. It selectively promotes certain genetic features that are considered beneficial to humanity. It is a selective form of procreation that rewards the more perfect, usually by also eliminating the less fortunate. It is a form of eugenics that has given eugenics its bad name.

Positive eugenics asserts that we should breed humans as we breed animals—and that we may kill them, as we kill animals. At the beginning of the previous century, this form of eugenics flourished, not only at universities and on the editorial boards of scientific journals, but also in politics. The Virginia Justice Oliver Wendell Holmes declared in Buck v. Bell (1927) that "three generations of imbeciles are enough," and launched a massive campaign of state-enforced sterilizations, thinking that America's salvation could be found in blocking the lower classes from breeding. Interestingly enough, the one dissenting vote to Holmes's decision was cast by the sole Catholic on the court, Pierce Butler.

Soon, eugenicists started giving IQ tests to Jewish immigrants on Ellis Island and reported that 40% of them were "feeble-minded"—in spite of the fact that they did not suffer from anything more than poverty and a lack of education. The 1924 *Immigration Act* drew heavily on ideas from eugenicists such as Madison Grant and Harry Laughlin. Eugenicists are made of the same cloth as KKK members, as both groups reject human equality; they consider some better than others, or at least claim that some should be treated better at the cost of others.

After its inception in the late 1800s, eugenics soon developed into a brutal movement which inflicted massive human rights violations on millions of people. The "interventions" advocated and practiced by eugenicists involved a wide range of "degenerates" or "unfits"—the poor, the blind, the mentally ill, entire "racial" groups such as Jews, Blacks, and Roma ("Gypsies"). All of these "misfits" were prevented from passing on their so-called defective traits. They were deemed "unfit" to live according to a despotic dogma of eugenicists called "survival of the fittest," which strives for the "racially pure"—Nietzsche's "Superman," Hitler's "Master Race," and KKK's "White Supremacists." This, in turn, led to practices such as segregation, sterilization, genocide, euthanasia, and pre-emptive abortions. The most extreme case is probably the Nazi ideology, which promoted the "superman" of the Arian race and suppressed the "degenerates" of Jews and Gypsies. George Bernard Shaw once predicted that "part of eugenic politics would finally land us in an extensive use of the lethal chamber."

An important propagandist of "positive eugenics" was the founder of the Planned Parenthood Federation of America: Margaret Higgins Sanger, a radical feminist, eugenicist, and Marxist—still the hero of many present-day abortion activists. Her statements, mostly published in her own magazine and some books, are horrendous, although mostly passed over by her followers nowadays. Here is a selection of her horrifying statements: "The most merciful thing that a large family does to one of its infant members is to kill it." The purpose in promoting birth control is "to create a race of thoroughbreds." "We do not want word to go out that we want to exterminate the Negro population." She also wrote that couples should be required to submit applications to have a child, for she detested the fact that "anyone, no matter how ignorant, how diseased mentally or physically, how lacking in all knowledge of children, seemed to consider he or she had the right to become a parent." It is hard to believe that all of this could ever have been put on paper, yet Planned Parenthood did not stray far from what its founder, Sanger, once proclaimed.

Where does this version of eugenics come from? Darwin may not have directly promoted eugenics, but he surely prepared the way for it. Indeed, his immediate family would soon become involved in that movement—his sons George and Leonard became active in promoting eugenics (Leonard serving as president of the Eugenics Education Society, the main eugenics group in Great Britain), and his cousin Francis Galton became the founder of the "eugenics crusade."

Unfortunately, the biological notion of "survival of the fittest" has indoctrinated many biologists and physicians to assess everything in terms of "winners" and "losers"—only the "fittest" are to survive at the cost of the weakest. Supporters of positive eugenics misguidedly jump from a descriptive notion ("genetically fit") to a prescriptive notion ("morally right"). They believe that, since genes are in control of our lives, they themselves should be in control of those genes. Yet persons with Down syndrome, or any other genetic "disorder," are only "misfits" or "losers" if we place the final end of human beings in their biological worth.

No matter how you look at it, these eugenicists have charged themselves with the grave duty to decide who is to live and who is to die—a quasi-moral stand based on purely biological grounds. One might tell these eugenicists that they are lucky to have been born already; having made it to the "boat," they are happy to shove other people back into the "water" by following their own, man-made "moral" laws. Instead, we need to keep stressing that no one has the right to claim that there are some human lives unworthy of living. Ironically, those who claim this right often fail to cope with many other equally important moral issues in life, whereas those who "should not qualify for life" may end up learning to cope with their medical adversity in unexpected and surprising ways.

No one has the right to judge the worth of someone else's life. What some call a curse may turn out to be a blessing. Each setback opens the prospect of a comeback. When a blind woman was asked how she could be so joyful, given her blindness, she responded with the question "How can you see and *not* be joyful?"

A well-known critic of positive eugenics was Pope Benedict XVI, who warned us of a new eugenics mentality on February 21, 2009. He condemned this "obsessive search for the 'perfect child,'" and added that "Man will always be greater than all that which makes up his body." Whereas eugenics places the final end of human beings in biological worth, Catholic teaching places it in eternal life. Put differently, the Church makes human culture subordinate to morality, whereas eugenics makes morality subject to cultural and political standards. When it comes to issues such as slavery, abortion, and genocide, eugenics only talks in terms of "winners" and "losers"; there is no longer talk of "good" and "bad," because those terms are not only outside its scope but are even declared illusory. That is why eugenics eventually dehumanizes, leading to what C. S. Lewis called "the abolition of man." As Pope John Paul II once observed, "When the sense of God is lost, there is also a tendency to lose the sense of man, of his dignity and life."

Interestingly enough, the man who discovered the cause of Down syndrome, Dr. Jérôme Lejeune, dedicated his entire career to protecting children with the syndrome in all manners at his disposal. In a similar vein, the later Surgeon General C. Everett Koop worked endlessly for children with congenital birth defects. In 1976, after spending an entire Saturday with his pediatric surgery team operating on three patients with severe congenital defects, Koop sat in the cafeteria and remarked that, together, they had given over two hundred years of life to three individuals who together barely weighed ten pounds.

Genetic Manipulation

We will not pay any attention to human cloning in this chapter, because there is no way that it can be morally justified. Yet it ranks high on the wish list of many scientists. Why? Unfortunately, bioscientists have been indoctrinated to look at life as a purely molecular phenomenon. Since molecules have no feelings and no morals, they can presumably be manipulated at the scientist's choosing, that is, without any restrictions. Although molecules will never protest, the *Catechism* (2294) does: "It is an illusion to claim moral neutrality in scientific research and its applications." Science cannot examine morality—it is beyond its reach—but morality should always be allowed to interrogate science. Let us move on to genetic manipulation.

Eugenics may have been dormant for a while, it seems, but it surely came alive again as the major ideology behind the so-called Reproductive Genetic Technologies (RGT), often connected with in vitro fertilization procedures (IVF). Here we have a new breed of eugenicists who urge parents to have the "best" children possible by using what they call a pre-implantation genetic diagnosis (PGD). In this procedure, a single cell is extracted from IVF embryos and then tested to see which embryos make the genetic cut. The embryos that "fail" the test are discarded or donated to research. The ones that "pass" have a chance to be transferred into a womb as a "designer baby." Some defend this kind of testing with the slogan "Man's power over Nature," but isn't that what C.S. Lewis calls "a power exercised by some men over other men with Nature as its instrument"? The moral problems with RGT are the same that we encounter with IVF.

Nowadays, a more "invasive" treatment has emerged: *gene therapy*. Gene therapy is the use of DNA as a pharmaceutical agent to correct the wrong allele and/or its protein product. Conditions that arise from mutations in a single gene are the best candidates for gene therapy. The most common form of gene therapy involves the insertion of a functional gene in the host genome at a specific location in the body. This is accomplished by isolating and copying the gene of interest, adding all the genetic elements for correct expression, and then inserting this assembly into the host organism. In order to get the therapeutic DNA inside the cell, the most common and successful method is the use of recombinant viruses by removing the viral DNA and then using the virus as a vehicle to deliver the therapeutic DNA.

The DNA that carries the code for a therapeutic protein is packaged within this "vector" and inserted into cells in the body. Once inside, the DNA becomes expressed by the cell machinery, resulting in the production of therapeutic protein, which in turn is supposed to cure the patient's disease. Unfortunately, there is always the fear that the viral vector or plasmid, once inside the patient, may recover its ability to cause disease. Besides, if the DNA is integrated in the wrong place in the genome—for example, in a tumor suppressor gene—it could induce a tumor.

Recently, there have been further developments in gene therapy. One of them is CRISPR (clustered regularly-interspaced short palindromic repeats). It typically also uses plasmids to reach the target cells. While we will not go into details regarding its mechanism, this technique does more than adding or replacing a complete gene at a random location in the cell; it can also delete and edit specific bits of DNA, even by changing a single base pair. One of its achievements is that it can snip out a mutated piece of DNA and replace it with the correct sequence. Obviously, the power of this technique can also become its danger.

The good news is there have been some success stories lately. Recent clinical successes include treatment of patients with chronic lymphocytic leukemia (CLL), acute lymphocytic leukemia (ALL), multiple myeloma, hemophilia, and Parkinson's disease. In all these cases, the therapeutic genes were transferred into the somatic cells (that is, not egg or sperm cells) of a patient. Therefore, any modifications and effects will be restricted to the individual patient only, and will not be inherited by the patient's offspring or later generations. On the other hand, benefits are usually short-term, so patients will have to undergo multiple rounds of gene therapy.

Because this therapy only affects the bodies of individual patients, and not future generations, it is called *somatic cell* gene therapy.

In addition, there is also *germ line* gene therapy, which modifies sperm cells or egg cells by the introduction of functional genes to be integrated into their genomes. This would allow the therapy to be hereditary, that is, passed on to later generations. Many countries (not the USA) prohibit this method for human beings because of technical and ethical concerns, most importantly insufficient knowledge about possible risks to future generations. Even the *somatic* version of gene therapy has many uncertainties and risks, including the risk that the new gene may cross the barrier between body and germ line by spreading to the testes or ovaries.

What is the Church's verdict on these techniques? It is not a complete rejection. The *Catechism* (2293) declares positively, "Basic scientific research, as well as applied research, is a significant expression of man's dominion over creation." The Catholic Church released further details in a 2008 document called *Dignitas Personae*. In it, the Church reinforces its continuing belief that a human being is sacred from conception, and no form of experimenting on embryos or use of embryonic stem cells is acceptable in any form. On the issue of Gene Therapy, it accepts that somatic cell gene therapy is, in principle, morally acceptable [*licit*], but states that germ line gene therapy (in its current form) is *not* acceptable because of risks to future children. An added problem with gene therapy applied to the embryo is the fact that it can only be done in the context of in vitro fertilization, and thus runs up against all the moral objections to such procedures. Therefore, it must be stated that, in its current state, germ line cell therapy in all its forms is morally unacceptable.

Another controversial issue in this context is stem-cell research. In the beginning, scientists made use of *embryonic* stem-cell lines (ESCs), but they were rejected by the patient as foreign entities— until it was technically possible to take the nucleus of an adult cell and insert it into an unfertilized egg, so that it would genetically match the patient. Technically, there are still many problems with ESCs. This makes the biologist Daniel Kuebler conclude, "ESC research seems to be stuck in neutral."

Ever since the first human *embryonic* stem cell lines were established in 1998, the Catholic Church has deemed this type of research morally unacceptable, because it requires the creation and subsequent destruction of human embryos. It does not matter whether scientific advances may result from it, for not everything that is biologically possible is morally permissible. The Church teaches that we may never intentionally do evil, even if good may come of it.

From the start, the Catholic Church has promoted *adult* stem cell lines (ASCs) instead of embryotic stem cell lines—and, curiously enough, only ASC-based therapies have displayed any type of therapeutic benefit. Unlike ESC therapies, ASC therapies have already reached the clinic and have benefited a multitude of patients. Fr. Tadeusz Pacholczyk makes a clear comparison: "Advocates are quick to point out that stem cell research is about helping those who are living. This is not quite correct. Only adult stem cell research is about helping the living. Embryonic stem cell research is about destructively harming some of the living, in the name of helping others who may be struggling with diseases." In 2010, the Vatican donated roughly $3 million to support researchers working with adult intestinal stem cells. Amazing how a Church that has had to say No to some biomedical developments knows very well when to say Yes to biomedical advances.

The Overpopulation Myth

Eugenics has not only been promoted for purposes of quality, but also for purposes of quantity: supposedly, there are too many people on Planet Earth. Eugenicists have been vigorous in spreading contraceptives and promoting abortion around the globe in order to combat what they call an imminent overpopulation. The allegation of overpopulation often lies behind movements for contraception, abortion, and sterilization. It is said that poverty, crime, hunger, pollution, and a host of other evils stem from having too many people in the world. Where does this idea come from?

Since the time of Thomas Malthus, who lived in the early 1800s, doomsayers have gloomily predicted that mankind would someday, even soon, outbreed its food supply, resulting in catastrophic famines. Malthus "proved" his predictions in this way: "Population, when unchecked, increases in a geometric ratio [*times* 2: 2-4-8-16-32, etc.]. Subsistence increases only in an arithmetic ratio [*plus* 2: 2-4-6-8-10, etc.]." In other words, in 1798 Thomas Malthus predicted that by 1890 the world would have standing room only. It must be said, however, that Malthus himself never advocated the coercive contraceptive approach that we associate with population planning today. Nonetheless, his doom prediction did gain traction. Nearly two centuries later, in the 1970s, media reports cautioned that by 1990 we would need to build huge artificial islands in the middle of the ocean to handle the earth's population. We are still waiting for that to happen.

To "prove" the undeniable power of geometric, or exponential, growth, there is a popular story about a pond partly covered with a growth of algae that doubles in size every day. The people living near the pond decide to wait to combat the algae until half the pond has been covered. How many days do they have left to take action? On the day that the pond is half covered, there is only one day left to take action, because the following day the pond will be completely covered. That surely looks very alarming and dramatic.

Comparisons like these usually have a counter-version. The panic story of an overgrown algae pond might be set against the story of the magic, never-ending pie (similar to the story of Achilles and the tortoise). Day after day, half of the pie is served. The pieces obviously get smaller and smaller each day, but the serving can go on forever—there is always a bit of pie left. The problem with mathematical puzzles like this one and the previous one is that they are about math, not reality. Everything depends on how one cuts the pie. Cutting the pie *in* pieces, the usual way, distributes all of the pie, but cutting pieces *off* the pie gives everyone a piece, for there is always an uncut piece left, no matter how small. Going back to our pond story, the pond is not only half full, but also half empty, so that, if the empty space is reduced by half each time, there will always be some space left for further growth. In other words, there are two sides to the story: a negative one and a positive one.

If we were to listen to Paul Ehrlich in his 1968 book *The Population Bomb*, we would hear only the negative version. We would see the earth as a lifeboat which is already full, and from which all new-comers must be pushed away. In his prologue, Ehrlich asserts, "The battle to feed all of humanity is over. In the 1970s hundreds of millions of people will starve to death in spite of any crash programs embarked upon now." He has yet to retract that statement.

Nevertheless, the ideas behind Ehrlich's book have brainwashed many. We hear the message in media and academia: "Having children is selfish." Or, "It's all about maintaining your genetic line at the expense of the planet." Or, "Never having a child is the most environmentally friendly thing one can do." Abortion activist Warren Hern described the human species as a "rapacious, predatory" organism displaying all the characteristics of a malignant tumor. In 1985, Planned Parenthood World Population circulated an article titled "The Human Race Has 35 Years Left: After that, People will Start Eating Plankton. Or People." 2020 must be the day of reckoning!

Obviously, these claims and statements call for a factual assessment as well as a moral assessment. Let us start with the facts. Thomas Malthus predicted that, by 1890, mankind would outbreed its food supply, resulting in catastrophic famines. Yet currently, 125 years later, the world produces enough food to feed 10 billion people—and there are "only" 7 billion of us. The predicted dates of massive food shortages due to overpopulation have all passed with no global famines—and with no apologies. They have passed because there is another "population power" that Malthus didn't factor in: brainpower. We have figured out ways to "produce subsistence" at a rate far greater than Malthus could ever imagine. Currently, scientists are even experimenting with how to create food in the lab. Someday, we may eat lab-burgers.

Those with a positive approach look forward to a world where more and more of the earth's resources will be brought into cultivation, and where the likelihood of finding more great men and women of genius is increased. But there are also those who prefer a negative approach, and who think and talk in terms of a population bomb ticking away until there is a population explosion. Their solution is to counteract this explosion with abortion. Yet by doing so, they destroy human capital, the ultimate resource of humanity.

Human ingenuity, it turns out, is the most precious resource we have—it is the motor that drives new discoveries and technological advances.

Apparently, the overpopulation slogan is a myth that has been growing overtime, ignoring the power of human ingenuity. When overpopulation activists bring up the issue of water shortage, they forget that we can do something about it. Lack of water is certainly a serious humanitarian issue, but it is not an overpopulation issue. Water, although plentiful, can be difficult to move to those who need it, which causes local water shortage. However, this calls for more ingenuity—more dams, canals, and pipelines, not more abortion, contraception and sterilizations. As Molly Yeh said, "The best tomato I ever had was a San Marzano picked straight from the plant—in the middle of the Negev desert." Israel is not alone in encouraging new farmers to grow in the desert; farming systems have been developed in desert hotspots such as Egypt, Australia, and southern California. Amazingly, water shortage can be cured with human ingenuity.

Something similar holds for food production. Contrary to Malthus's prediction, food production has exceeded population growth, as better farming techniques have allowed producers to produce more food on less land. According to the Food and Agriculture Organization of the United Nations (2009), the world produces more than 1½ times enough food to feed everyone on the planet. There is no reason to think that we are running out of human ingenuity and technological advances. If anything, a larger population means more opportunities for the kind of scientific collaboration and increased specialization that results in such scientific leaps forward. According to the World Education Service, "world agriculture produces 17% more calories per person today than it did 30 years ago." Economists Peter Bauer and Basil Yamey of the London School of Economics discovered that the population scare "relies on misleading statistics . . . misunderstands the determinants of economic progress . . . misinterprets the causalities in changes in fertility and changes in income."

So what are the real facts? The writer Helen M. Valois gives us a good assessment:

There are approximately 52.5 million square miles of land in the world, not including Antarctica. In 1997, the world's population was 5.9 billion. By allowing 3.5 square feet per person, all the people in the world could be brought together in an area the size of the city of Jacksonville, Florida. While everyone would admittedly be cramped in Jacksonville, it would be possible to allot each individual person 1,000 square feet (4,000 square feet of living space for a family of four) and still fit the entire world's population in the states of Nebraska, Kansas, and South Dakota, leaving the rest of the United States, plus Canada, Mexico, Central and South America, Europe, Africa, Asia, and the Australian South Pacific areas completely uninhabited by man.

Much of the following information was researched by population experts Steven W. Mosher and Anne Roback Morse. The idea that half of all people who have ever lived are currently alive turns out to be a myth as well. Demographers estimate that at least 20 billion people lived on earth between the years 8000 B.C. and the birth of Christ. The ongoing myth of overpopulation is actually a cluster of myths, some statistical, some philosophical, and some spiritual. The population of the world doubled from 3 billion in 1960 to 6 billion in 2000—not because we were reproducing more quickly, but because the death rate had dramatically slowed during this time thanks to advances in modern medicine.

The fertility rate had also gone down—another factor Malthus had forgotten or could not anticipate. The reasons are manifold: more women were using contraception (natural or artificial); more adults were unmarried; more women delayed their first pregnancy; more governments promoted or enforced abortion. The global total fertility rate is currently 2.53 children per woman. In 1960 it was an average of 6 children per woman, by 1995 it was down to 3 per woman, and by 2002 it was just 2.6. A rate of around 2.1 is the replacement level—that is, the number of children that each couple needs to have to maintain the population. (The extra one-tenth accounts for those who do not have children.) Overpopulation activists would applaud all of this. But is it really good news?

About 48% of all people live in a country with below-replacement fertility. In areas such as China, children are being forcefully killed to reduce population growth, while inhabitants of other countries are led to believe that it is their duty not to have children. At the current rate, about half the countries of Europe, for example, would lose 95% or more of their population. Very low fertility levels lead not only to population decline, but also to rapid population ageing. Fewer babies today means fewer workers tomorrow, and, therefore, greater difficulties in sustaining production. Governments can produce a lot, but they cannot reproduce—so they should stay away from preventing reproduction. The fact is that, rather than a booming population, we now have an aging population—elderly people may soon outnumber young people.

What has happened to the overpopulation myths? Overpopulation describes a situation in which the number of people exhausts the resources in a closed environment, such that it can no longer support that population—which is not our case. Overpopulation is a matter of numbers, and does not reflect how people live. If every person demanded his or her own continent or island, the world would indeed seem "overpopulated" very quickly. What we find today is rather "over-concentration" or "over-crowding," not overpopulation. There is plenty of room for people who choose to move; in fact, if they were properly spaced, every man, woman, and child on earth could have 5 acres of land. But somehow, many people prefer densely populated cities over a less-populated countryside. Ironically, some city people are more concerned about the number of people than the number of pets on the planet; they add to the population size and the demand for food by wanting to own dogs and cats. The overpopulation myth does not seem to stop the growing number of pets.

To counter the overpopulation myth, the Population Research Institute announced in 1999, "We are grateful that Baby Six Billion has come into the world. Baby Six Billion, boy or girl, red or yellow, black or white, is not a liability, but an asset. Not a curse, but a blessing. For all of us." The threat of "overpopulation" is political hype, similar to the hype which claims that climate change is entirely man-made. Sure, it would probably be nice to have a little more elbow room in supermarkets, or less traffic during our morning commute, but we cannot call that overpopulation. The claims of the Zero Population Growth (ZPG) lobby are perhaps "politically correct," but they crumble when confronted with the facts.

In addition to the factual assessment given above, we need a moral assessment. Parents have a natural right to determine the size of their families. The number of children in a family is a decision for parents alone to make, depending on their financial situation and on whether the mother can handle another pregnancy. The *Catechism* (2368) puts it this way: "For just reasons, spouses may wish to space the births of their children." The state cannot make this decision for them. In fact, the size of the family is not an issue of morality at all—openness to children and responsible family planning are. Parents determine the size of their family on the basis of spiritual, economic, social, and, most of all, moral responsibilities.

Yet that is not how the overpopulation lobby sees it. As a newspaper advertisement reproduced in abortion-activist Lawrence Lader's *Breeding Ourselves to Death* once put it, "Every 8 seconds a new American is born. He is a disarming little thing, but he begins to scream loudly in a voice that can be heard for seventy years. He is screaming for 56,000,000 gallons of water, 21,000 gallons of gasoline, 10,150 pounds of meat, 28,000 pounds of milk and cream, 9,000 pounds of wheat, and great storehouses of all other foods, drinks, and tobaccos." The agenda of the overpopulation activist is clear: to control the rate of new births. Every new birth is considered a menace to humanity. As the authors Leon J. Suprenant and Philip C. L. Gray remark, "No mention is made of the fact that this same child will also grow up to be a producer and contribute to society in tangible and intangible ways."

It was, again, Margaret Sanger, founder of the American Eugenics League, who put the "control" in "birth control." Desiring to stem the tide of "teeming, unwanted, and unnecessary pregnancies," she helped popularize abortion, contraception, and sterilization during the early part of the previous century. She was soon followed by what Tom Hoopes calls the "Contraceptive Imperialists," who have decided that "the best way to help poor people feed children is to eliminate children needing to be fed, and that the cheapest way to care for the poor is for the poor to not exist to have to be bothered with." These ideologues, and many others supporting them, have given their methods of spreading contraceptives and promoting abortion the clean and neutral label of "birth control."

Dr. Jacqueline Kasun, professor of economics at Humboldt State University in Arcata, CA, has exposed the role of Planned Parenthood, International Planned Parenthood, and many of its affiliates in aggressively curtailing live births because of overpopulation. According to her, abortion has been promoted by Planned Parenthood among teenagers in public schools, among minority groups in community "health centers," and especially among the poor. Already much of US aid to foreign countries has birth-control requirements. We must ask ourselves on what grounds a government may demand, as a condition for receiving American aid, that a country reduce the size of its families to an average of two children. Yet this is what is happening now; in Africa, for instance, with its fast-growing population, many official agencies constantly and aggressively push contraceptives and abortion, which made Pope Francis speak of an "ideological colonization."

It must be apparent by now that the Catholic Church cannot support any of these policies. Pope John Paul II made this very clear when he said, "It is therefore morally unacceptable to encourage, let alone impose, the use of methods such as contraception, sterilization, and abortion in order to regulate births." He actually repeated what Pope Pius XII had said decades earlier:

> So overpopulation is not a valid reason for spreading illicit birth control practices. It is simply a pretext used by those who would justify avarice and selfishness—by those nations, for instance, who fear that the expansion of others will pose a danger to their own political position and cause a lowering of the general standard of living, or by individuals, especially those who are better off, who prefer the greatest possible enjoyment of earthly goods to the praise and merit of bringing new lives into existence.

While the birth-control activists see and analyze the world in "population" terms, Christians know that a population is, first of all, a group—however large—of "individuals." Each one of them is gifted by God with an immortal soul, endowed with rationality and morality. Each is made in God's image and likeness—the priceless value of each human being. While birth control activists regard a baby as a waste of good food and resources, the Christian knows that sustaining human life is what food and resources are for. Sometimes we need to see the trees for the forest, instead of the other way around.

Helen Valois clarifies further: "Proponents of population control are not arguing that there are too many people in the world. They are arguing that there are too many *other* people in the world. True to their eugenic roots, population alarmists divide the human race into the valuable part, which deserves to live, and the worthless part, which doesn't." G. K. Chesterton had expressed this much earlier: "The answer to anyone who talks about the surplus population is to ask him whether he is the surplus population; or if not, how he knows he is not."

There is an old anecdote about a zealot of population control attending a penthouse cocktail party. Holding forth at eloquent length on the need to reduce the number of people in the world, he was interrupted in his monologue by the hostess, who graciously ushered him to a nearby window. "If there are too many people in the world," she smiled, "why don't you set an example and go first?"

7

Sex and Gender Change

L et us find out first what determines whether the new organism growing in its mother's womb will be a female or a male. Human beings carry 23 pairs of matching chromosomes, of which one pair is an "unmatched" pair of sex chromosomes in males (XY), while a "real" pair (XX) in females. For procreation, it is necessary that males produce sperm cells—each one having a half, unpaired set of 22 chromosomes plus either an X or a Y chromosome—and that females release egg cells, again with a half, unpaired set of 22 chromosome, but this time always combined with an X chromosome. The egg cell always carries one X chromosome, but the sperm cell can introduce either an X or a Y chromosome. If the egg is fertilized by a Y-bearing sperm cell, the new organism will develop into a male (XY), but if it is fertilized is by an X-bearing sperm cell, the new organism will develop into a female (XX).

The Biology behind It

A baby's sex is basically determined at the time of conception. Sex is a "genetic" issue in a rather odd sense; whereas tall parents may have tall children, and short parents may have short children, every girl or every boy has exactly one parent of each sex. Because the number of X-bearing and Y-bearing sperm cells should be fifty-fifty, we expect a 1:1 sex ratio. In fact, there are slight deviations from this expectation at birth. In almost all human populations, there is a small excess of males at birth—about 106 boys are born for every 100 girls. Part of the explanation might be a small difference in the ability of X-bearing and Y-bearing sperm cells to fertilize egg cells, plus a small difference in prenatal mortality rates between male and female fetuses.

Apparently, the human Y chromosome carries genes with strong male-determining properties; it is the absence of a Y chromosome that determines femaleness. However, it is not just the Y chromosome itself that is the determining factor, but rather the *SRY* gene on the Y chromosome which acts as a master switch and is responsible for the development of an unborn baby into a male by initiating the testes development (whereas other genes on the Y chromosome are important for male fertility). When this *SRY* gene is present, early embryonic testes develop around the 10th week of pregnancy. In the absence of both the *SRY* gene and a testis-determining factor (*TDF*), ovaries develop. In general, one could say that sex determination of a male depends on the testes, and testis differentiation depends on the Y chromosome and its *SRY* and *TDF* genes.

In the early developmental stages, the genitalia of males and females are virtually identical. Whether these structures will become female or male depends on the presence of the male hormone testosterone during this critical stage of development—in particular di-hydro-testosterone (*DHT*), a derivative of testosterone. Key to this is a functional *SRY* gene. If this gene is defective, testes do not develop; without testes, no testosterone is produced; without testosterone, no internal male organs are formed; consequently, the external genitalia become female genitalia.

Although, technically speaking, it is not the Y chromosome but rather the *SRY* gene on the Y chromosome that determines maleness, it is still fair to say that being male or female was determined at the moment of fertilization. From then on, development is "steered" in one of two directions. At the 10th week, the penis of the male is slightly larger than the clitoris of the female. At the 12th week, the male scrotum has formed from the tissue that becomes the labia major in the female. Finally, at the 34th week, the distinctive features of the genitalia of the two sexes are fully present. Therefore, at birth, the anatomical differences between male and female are rather unambiguous.

After birth, other sex-related differences kick in. Particularly when puberty sets in, the differences between the two sexes become much more prominent. Puberty is a period of several years in which rapid physical growth and psychological changes occur, culminating in sexual maturity. The average onset of puberty is at age 10 or 11 for girls and age 12 or 13 for boys—but there seems to be a trend towards an earlier start. Puberty begins with a surge in hormone production, which, in turn, causes a number of physical changes. It is a stage of life in which a child develops its so-called secondary sex characteristics—for example, a deeper voice and larger Adam's apple in boys, and development of breasts and more curved and prominent hips in girls. These changes are triggered by the pituitary gland, which secretes a surge of hormonal agents into the blood stream, initiating a chain reaction. The male and female sex glands (gonads) are subsequently activated, which puts them into a state of rapid growth and development; as a consequence, the testes primarily release testosterone, and the ovaries predominantly dispense estrogen. The production of these hormones increases gradually until sexual maturation has been reached.

All these biological changes are directly or indirectly sex-related. But once the newborn has been "declared" a boy or a girl at birth, based on anatomical and sexual characteristics, much more is going to happen. This particular aspect of development is usually captured with the term *gender*. Whereas sex is ingrained in our nature, gender is acquired, partly based on cultural restrictions, partly on personal choices. This distinction between sex and gender is generally accepted nowadays. According to the *World Health Organization*, sex refers to the biological and physiological characteristics that define men and women, whereas gender refers to the socially constructed roles, behaviors, activities, and attributes that a given society considers appropriate for men and women.

A difference in gender entails much more than a difference in biological characteristics—namely, differences in behavioral traits, social roles, and cultural expectations that come with being a man or a woman. Early on in human development, parents as well as society take on a "molding" role. As soon as parents know that their child is a boy, for instance, they tend to treat it as a boy, which makes the child consider himself as of the male gender. There seems to be an extended process that runs from genes to sex, and from sex to gender. During this process, children develop their identity in interaction with their parents. Parents are complementary to each other; some like to say that men are from Mars and women are from Venus. It is in this environment of complementary features that children develop their own identity.

Apparently, the gender of a person is much farther away from a person's genes than the sex of a person. This is why we make the distinction between sex and gender. On the "way" to gender, there are many inroads from the environment—the impact of upbringing, peers, and cultural expectations. This may partly explain why girls can differ in femininity and boys in masculinity. Whereas sex differences are "inborn," gender differences appear to be more "acquired," "taught," or even "self-taught." In other words, the terms "male" and "female" are sex categories, while the labels "masculine" and "feminine" are gender categories. Pope John Paul II put this in a wider context: When Adam and Eve saw each other, they realized that there are "two complementary ways of being conscious of the meaning of the body." This is how they discovered masculinity and femininity.

It needs to be stated again: Whereas sex is heavily dependent on "inside" factors such as genes, gender is not; gender relies heavily on "outside" factors coming from the environment. When growing up, we often follow habits acquired at home, in school, through peers and friends, and through the society we live in—and that is also true about gender. This is not to say that gender has nothing to do with genes, but gender, more often than not, may be a matter of lifestyle choices rather than the outcome of a set of genetic instructions.

Hopes, dreams, and expectations have a strong impact on the way a person develops. It is often hard to determine how people became who they are; perhaps they were "born" that way, perhaps they were "made" that way, or maybe they "chose" to be that way. If teachers falsely tell their students that genetic research has shown that the allele for a blue eye color also positively affects intelligence, you can almost bank on the probability that blue-eyed students will soon perform better in class, without any genetic input. It is a self-fulfilling prophecy.

This distinction between sex and gender is important to keep in mind. For example, when we talk about homosexuality, we are talking in terms of gender. Homosexuality is not a change in sex—of producing either egg cells or sperm cells—but rather a matter of gender, which suggests that it is many steps away from the genes we carry, and thus allows for many inroads from the environment as well. Even if one were to argue that genes affect hormones, that hormones affect the brain, and that the brain affects one's behavior, we should emphasize that this behavior, in turn, affects the brain. A similar phenomenon is well known in sports: strong muscles benefit those who play sports, but playing sports, in turn, greatly benefits the development of the muscles.

Based on the distinction between sex and gender, we can see more clearly what the difference is between males and females. Consider the following trivial examples. In certain cultures, once originated in Persia, males wear trousers, whereas tunics and robes are more typical among Muslims and ancient Greeks or Romans. Traditionally, females have usually worn skirts and robes, but nowadays they increasingly wear jeans. Earrings are common among females in our culture, but they are now also chosen by some males. The army used to be for males, but in many countries it is now open to females. CEOs used to be recruited from among males, but are now increasingly found among females. Firefighting is no longer an exclusively masculine activity, and nursing is no longer an entirely feminine activity. The list could go on and on. The only boundary that cannot be crossed is the child-bearing capacity of females and their sexual organs. In other words, there is not much that is intrinsic about gender, but sex is intrinsic. Gender is pliable, but sex is not. Yet, ultimately, both go back to two chromosomes—XX or XY—which are received at conception.

The Morality behind It

So far, things seem to be rather straightforward. But there is a darker side to the sex-gender distinction. Using the gender concept sometimes obscures the reality of sex differences, making us believe that we can manipulate things entirely to our own liking. This idea has given certain activist movements an alibi to reject the binary division of persons into two sexes, so that they can claim the freedom to be either, both, or neither, depending on their mood.

However, the fact remains that gender does not and cannot replace or alter sex. Male and female roles certainly have a social and cultural component, but they still reflect inherent biological differences between the sexes. When a baby is born, the obstetrician or midwife announces, "It's a boy" or "It's a girl"—and it will stay that way. Therefore, gender is not the sex a person decides to identify with; instead, it is a further implementation of the finer details of a person's given sex and personality. It allows for a broader scale, albeit within the dichotomy of the two sexes. The gender of members of the female sex can be more or less feminine, while the gender of those of the male sex can be more or less masculine. In the meantime, the dichotomy of male and female remains standing.

But that is not the way things stand in the *transgender* debate. There are "gender ideologists" who want us to believe that we are not born as "F" or "M" but "X," so that we can then later decide whether we want to be "F," "M," or anything in between. This belies the plain fact that persons whose biological sex is male cannot have a female trans-gender identity; if they think that they do, it is only an imitation of their personal conception of the other sex. This "gender ideology" destroys a person's identity as a man or a woman. Your sex is supposedly no longer something you were born with, but something declared on your birth certificate. Relativists tell us that we live in a world of "social constructions." If John says he is a women, then John is a woman—that is a matter of fairness. But isn't fairness, then, also a "social construct," making fairness no better than unfairness?

Instead, we must acknowledge that sex is not a social construction but a biological one. Gender ideologists try to obscure this idea by speaking of "sexual orientation," which is a rather vague term that includes things as different as sexual desire, sexual attraction, and patterns of sexual behavior. The underlying idea is as follows: Whatever you say you are, you are. As Professor David Carlin puts it, "If there is no objective truth, we are free to believe whatever we like, including utter nonsense." In this case, sex is the "objective truth," gender is not.

Not surprisingly, some people in the medical field have constructed a syndrome they call a "gender identity disorder." Labels like these are presumptuous; they tend to give things the allure of objectivity and reality. It is this gender ideology that makes some believe that same-sex relationships are "natural." Yet the reality of the two sexes should make them realize that reproduction still requires a person of the other sex. What previous generations took for granted—that words such as *man, woman, mother,* and *father* name natural realities as well as social roles—is now increasingly regarded as obsolete.

Strange as it may sound, the gender ideology, in essence, rejects the gender concept. At its most basic level, the gender concept simply asserts that "sex" and "gender" are not identical. But then, gender ideologists reject that distinction. They have—sometimes openly, sometimes slyly—changed the definition of the gender concept. They have redefined "gender" to refer to *the sex a person identifies with.* If a male identifies with the female sex, they say, that must be his, or now her, "real" sex, so doctors must make it come true. In the minds of many, your natural, God-given sexual biology is less relevant to who you are than is the gender identity you have chosen to assume.

In 2012, Pope Benedict XVI addressed the gender issue. He connected an extreme version of the gender theory with the words of the French philosopher Simone de Beauvoir: "one is not born a woman, one becomes so"—in denial of the fact that one is born as a woman, but may not think so. Taken this way, the pontiff declared the "gender" ideology a new philosophy of sexuality: "According to this philosophy, sex is no longer a given element of nature, that man has to accept and personally make sense of: it is a social role that we choose for ourselves, while in the past it was chosen for us by society." The Pontiff was basically asserting that this version of gender theory confuses sex with gender, and thus confuses sexual identity with gender identity.

Instead, it must be stated that sexual identity refers to *being* male or female. In the words of the *Catechism* (2333), "Everyone, man and woman, should acknowledge and accept his sexual identity." For example, men cannot, as males, bear or gestate children, as they do not have such a capacity, but women do. Thus, being male or female is essential to who and what a person is. It is, in essence, determined at the moment of conception—XX or XY. Gender, on the other hand, refers to certain emotional, psychological, cultural, and social dispositions or traits more characteristic of femininity or masculinity. Once we understand this distinction, gender is pliable, but sex is not and therefore cannot be changed.

In other words, we are either male or female persons, and nothing can change that fact—but we may be more or less feminine or masculine. A person's body is a fundamental indication of what sex he or she belongs to. It is a physical, empirically verifiable reality that does not change simply because our beliefs or desires do. One can mutilate one's genitals, but one cannot change one's sex. One can change what genitalia and gonads one was born with, but not one's sex. You cannot "re-invent" yourself that way, because you never "invented" yourself to begin with.

True, if the human body were merely a machine, without a soul or spirit, we could alter the body and "fix" it as we would a car or an appliance. For many people today, the human body belongs to the one who "has" it as property. Thus, the human body becomes an object—a thing that is owned, like a machine. If the human body were a machine, and not the expression of the human person, many things would be possible. For example, we could rent it out, as in prostitution; we could claim it, as in rape. But since a human body is not a machine, any actions that treat it as a machine should be morally rejected.

Nevertheless, biology tends to isolate the body from the person, in spite of the fact that the body and soul is always a person's body. The same should be said about the soul—it is always a person's soul. Ultimately, we cannot separate the body from a person nor can we treat the soul as separate from a person. Although we can mentally distinguish between our bodies and our souls, that does not make them divisible in practice. The fact that we can distinguish a flame's heat from its light does not mean that we can separate the heat from the light. Yet, since Descartes, we have tended not only to separate body and soul, but to set them against each other in an antagonistic relationship—a master/slave relationship, so to speak. Consequently, the body is often seen as a prison from which the soul wants to escape. However, a human being is not merely a body or machine—he or she is a body with a soul, a person. Neither is a human being merely a soul. It is not so that the soul is enslaved by the flesh, neither is the body ruled by a tyrannical soul.

The tendency to disconnect body and soul leads to dangerous consequences, such as the separation between sex and love, or between procreation and marriage. It also makes some people decide to undergo sex-change surgery because they feel that their soul is "trapped" in the body of the opposite sex. Cases like these set the soul in opposition to the body, based on the mistaken belief that only the soul and mind are considered the "real me," thus leaving the body at the mercy of the soul. In this view, an entirely isolated soul can decide on its own what the body should be, male or female. What is lost in this approach is the fact that body and soul are a unity, with the soul expressing itself through the body. Obviously, transgender or transsexual activists deny this truth. First they disrupt the unity between body and soul, and then they create a disconnect between the two. There is no such thing as a disembodied soul. There is no such thing as a female soul trapped in a male body, or reversed.

What does this mean for the transgender debate? Receiving hormones of the opposite sex and surgically removing genitalia or gonads are not sufficient to change one's sex. In 1979, after commissioning a study of the outcomes of sex-change operations, Dr. Paul McHugh in his capacity as chair of the Department of Psychiatry, put a halt to transsexual surgery at Johns Hopkins Hospital. He wrote, "We psychiatrists, I thought, would do better to concentrate on trying to fix their minds and not their genitalia." McHugh compares medical treatment of patients with confused gender identity to treating anorexia with liposuction. He calls transgendered individuals "feminized men or masculinized women, counterfeits or impersonators of the sex with which they 'identify.'"

This may explain why the so-called "gender-identity disorder" is on the rise; it seems to have become epidemic. The physician and philosopher Carl Elliott, MD, was right when he said that cultural and historical conditions have not just revealed transsexuals, but may actually be creating them. It has become a "disorder" we have no further control of, yet it is a "disorder" created out of thin air. Because of an increasing number of broken families and same-sex parents, the right parent may not be available for the child to identify with, and therefore its gender may not have a chance to line up with the appropriate sex. As the lawyer Joseph Backholm said about transgender activists, "The irony is that a sex change itself reinforces the gender stereotypes they claim to be rejecting."

As a matter of fact, transsexual individuals could be compared to transracial individuals. There are many similarities. In either case, it is a *decision* to changeover. We had a recent case of someone who claimed a "transracial identity," in a way similar to claims of a transsexual identity. This sparked a conversation that we did not even know we needed to have. Is it really possible for an individual to be born "in the wrong skin"? There is the soul-body separation again. Even if you identify closely with the Black community, that does not make you a person of African descent.

Something similar could be said about transsexual or transgender individuals. In either case, proponents of transition are quick to claim that they want to redefine "traditional labels" of sexuality, inspiring some to do the same with ethnicity. Yet perception does not change reality. Transgendered men do not become women, nor do transgendered women become men; our sex is part of who we are—just as transracial individuals do not become members of another race by perception, because their skin color is a part of who they are. A man declaring that he is a woman is just as odd as a white woman declaring that she is "actually" black.

Let's unite body and soul again by being happy in our bodies. The *Catechism* (2393) states, "By creating the human being man and woman, God gives personal dignity equally to the one and the other. Masculinity and femininity are complementary—different but equal expressions of what it is to be human. Each of them, man and woman, should acknowledge and accept his sexual identity." Interestingly enough, it was through each other that Adam and Eve discovered their own identity.

Peter Kreeft seems to have been right on target when he remarked, about the words "masculinity" and "femininity," that

> [They] have been reduced from archetypes to stereotypes. [...] The main fault in the old stereotypes was their too-tight connection between sexual being and social doing, their tying of sexual identity to social roles, especially for women: the feeling that it was somehow unfeminine to be a doctor, lawyer, or politician. But the antidote to this illness is not confusing sexual identities but locating them in our being rather than in our doing.

A recent report by Dr. Lawrence Mayer and Dr. Paul McHugh based on nearly 200 peer-reviewed studies of sexual orientation and gender identity, discloses some striking information. First, only a minority of children who express gender-atypical thoughts or behavior will continue to do so into adolescence or adulthood. Second, among transgender individuals, 41% have attempted suicide, whereas only 4.6% of the overall US population reports "a lifetime suicide attempt." The hypothesis of "social stress" as an explanation has so far not been corroborated. Third, one hospital's practice of surgically removing the poorly-developed genitalia of male infants and giving them female genitalia showed that, years later, most of the subjects still identified as male, although their parents had been directed to raise the boys as girls.

Nevertheless, the transgender issue has become so politicized that it has even invaded the restrooms, locker-rooms, and shower facilities of schools in the United States of America. In the name of anti-discrimination rhetoric, transgender individuals must be allowed access to the facilities consistent with their "gender identity." The irony is that this creates a new form of discrimination: it discriminates on the basis of and in favor of gender identity. As the lawyer Edward Whelan, President of the Ethics and Public Policy Center, puts it, "It makes gender identity determine which restrooms and showers a person is allowed to use, just as a policy of race segregated restrooms and showers makes race determine which facilities a person is allowed to use." And then he asks, "How could one of the males be allowed to use the girls' facilities and the other be barred from doing so?" If transgender people truly want "equal protection under the law," they cannot expect to be treated as a separate class of people, distinct from the rest of society.

Unfortunately, psychiatrists have powerful voices in this discussion. They have claimed the "authority" to decide whether the transgender issue is "real." They are supposed to speak in the name of science, so many people bow their heads in obedience. However, the problem with psychiatry is that its practitioners often try to disguise their personal convictions and opinions as scientific facts. Psychiatry is arguably the least science-based branch of the medical specialties; some experts do not even consider it a science. It is very susceptible to philosophical, ideological, and religious viewpoints—probably because its field of study is very close to those territories. Because of this, it exposes itself to contamination, and thus to criticism.

The psychiatrist Thomas Szasz goes as far as rejecting the whole concept of mental illness; he considers it a plot to interfere with a person's human rights—a "science of lies," as he calls it. Nevertheless, all professionals in mental health in general, and psychiatry in particular, should take the time to look at their own preconceptions, actions, statements, and morals. It is frightening to see how much decisive power psychiatrists have in our healthcare system and judicial system. But if we feel ourselves to be at their mercy, that is something we bring on ourselves.

Homosexuality

Another gender-related issue is homosexuality, although some prefer to speak of "sexual orientation"—a sexual attraction toward persons of the other sex, or the same sex. Homosexuality is certainly not a matter of sex, let alone a change in sex, for homosexuals are either males (gays) who produce sperm cells in their testicles or females (lesbians) who produce egg cells in their ovaries. Therefore, homosexuality must be a matter of gender, which suggests that it is somewhat farther away from the impact of genes and DNA, and hence allows for many inroads from the environment. Many possible factors have been theorized; they range widely from high levels of certain hormones in the mother's body during pregnancy to excessive maternal care during childhood.

There have been many trials intended to anchor homosexuality in genetics, but none of them are very convincing. In contrast, a 1991 study of identical twins showed that 52% (29 pairs out of 56) of the identical twins in the study were both homosexual; 22% (12 pairs out of 54) of the fraternal twins were both homosexual; and 11% (6 of 57) of the adoptive brothers where both homosexual. If homosexuality is genetically determined, why did only 52% of the identical twins share the same sexual orientation? The question arises of what to make of the other 48% of the twins who differed in their sexual orientation. What other factors could foster same-sex attraction? Several causal links have been mentioned. Possible causes could be the experience of sexual abuse as a child or bullying by peers. According to a 2011 meta-analysis of 37 North American studies, non-heterosexuals were 2.9 times more likely to report sexual abuse as children, and non-heterosexuals were 1.7 times more likely to have been attacked or threatened by their peers.

Let's face it—we don't really know what causes homosexuality. The *Catechism* (2357) has it right: "Its psychological genesis remains largely unexplained." The ongoing search for genes that are believed to determine homosexuality is controversial; it is a search for something that may have nothing to do with genes. In comparison, it is hard to believe that there is such a thing as a "chip gene" for people with an addiction to chips, a "chocolate gene" for chocoholics, or a "spending gene" for habitual big spenders. The field of behavioral genetics is littered with failed links between particular genes and certain behavioral traits. We are constantly being bombarded with new genes: a gene for alcohol addiction, a gene for homosexuality, a gene for schizophrenia, a gene for altruism, and even a gene for religion.

Reacting to the casual way in which some neurobiologists speak of a gene for depression or a gene for violence, for example, one could argue that depression and violence are only labels for rather complicated and variable patterns of behavior. The hypothetical genes some have come up with were once claimed, and then had to be retracted; they were often inventions in a scientist's mind that did not lead to discoveries in reality. This may also be true of homosexuality: the search for a gene is still on, but it may never be fully settled.

This is not to say that all of the above inventions are bogus, but most of them are still in the stage of invention and are awaiting the stage of discovery. Perhaps alcoholism is not genetic, but rather something acquired at home, in the womb, or in a group of peers. Perhaps pedophilia is not an issue of genetics but rather a form of immoral behavior—rape, that is. Perhaps Munchausen Syndrome is only a cry for attention or sympathy. Human behavior may be, more often than not, a matter of lifestyle choices rather than the outcome of a set of genetic instructions. Even if there are genes that determine a certain behavior, we need to realize that genes often must be "turned on" by an outside force before they can do their "preprogrammed" job.

As a consequence, it is extremely difficult to link genes to personality—so difficult, in fact, that no one has done it yet. To put it differently, there is not a gene for everything. If you never touch alcohol or illegal drugs, you will never develop an addiction to these substances. If you did touch them, though, would you be led by a genetic compulsion or rather by peer pressure, a sense of depression, or even mere curiosity? Probably any or all of the above.

Even if homosexuality someday turns out to have a genetic basis, such a biological verdict does not necessarily wipe out any moral considerations. Earlier, we said that biological criteria do not automatically qualify as moral criteria. Even if there is, for instance, a genetic basis for kleptomania or violence, that does not mean that the moral issue of theft or murder is out of the question. It is much more likely that morality has priority over what genes dictate than that genes control morality.

Genetic determinism does not and cannot wipe out morality. Instead, we could make the case that the idea of genetic determinism is invented as one giant alibi for moral responsibility. Once we declare ourselves no longer responsible for our moral decisions, we think that we are off the moral hook. If we wish to be innocent, we must find a way to make the claim that we cannot be held morally responsible. So some have indeed found a way: that of "geneticizing" or "psychologizing" bad moral behavior, so that the victimizer is no longer a person, but a pathology caused by genes—a "disease" supposedly beyond our moral control.

Once we have made ourselves victims, we feel released from moral responsibility, since victims are, by definition, not responsible for their conditions, but can point instead to something else as the culprit—genes, hormones, diseases, syndromes, and pathologies. The new line of defense is: "My genes made me do it!" Morality, on the other hand, invites us to be more *self*-determined and less *pre*-determined. It tells us not to make excuses, but to make commitments. One of those commitments is acceptance of one's sexual identity. As the *Catechism* (2333) puts it, "Everyone, man and woman, should acknowledge and accept his sexual identity."

Medicalization has also been attempted for homosexuality. Freud had already concluded that paranoia and homosexuality were inseparable. The American Psychiatric Association (APA) considered homosexuality a mental illness until 1974. In 1970, gay activists protested against the APA convention in San Francisco, so in 1973 the APA recommended that homosexuality be declared "normal," although only 58% of the members who voted favored the change. What is noteworthy about this is that there was no new fact or set of facts that motivated this major change; instead, it was the power of the gay lobby that initiated the revision. The psychologist Philip Hickey worded it this way, "So all the people who had this terrible 'illness' were 'cured' overnight—by a vote!"

As an interesting side note, four years later, in 1977, ten thousand members of the APA were polled at random, asking them their opinion on this issue. *Time Magazine* summarized the results of the poll: 69% said that they believed "homosexuality is usually a pathological adaptation," 18% disagreed, and 13% were uncertain. In the meantime, the gay lobby keeps working hard to further change these numbers in their favor. Its goal is to cause a shift in what is considered "politically correct." One thing is clear: this development has nothing to do with advances in science.

Regardless of these social, cultural, and political developments, we still have to face the question of how to evaluate homosexuality in a *moral* way. The natural law is our moral compass, for it tells us where to go and where not to go. Somehow we have lost sight of what nature intended; we seem to know the purpose of every part of our bodies—except our genitals. We have also lost sight of what nature did *not* intend: Instead of a mutual self-giving in spousal love, homosexual intercourse is a *utilization* of each other's body. It is a man's using another man as a woman, and a woman's using another woman as a man. This may explain why homosexual men keep searching for satisfaction that they cannot reach. The scientists Bell and Weinberg, for instance, reported evidence of widespread sexual compulsion among homosexual men. 83% of the homosexual men surveyed estimated they had had sex with 50 or more partners in their lifetime, 43% estimated they had had sex with 500 or more partners; 28% with 1,000 or more partners.

What, then, is so "unnatural"—that is, in violation of what nature intended—about homosexuality, especially male homosexuality? Anal intercourse is the *sine qua non* of sex for many gay men. Yet human physiology makes it clear that the body was not designed to accommodate this activity. The rectum is significantly different from the vagina with regard to suitability for penetration by a penis. The vagina has natural lubricants—aroused by love-making—and is supported by a network of muscles. It is composed of a mucus membrane with a multi-layer stratified squamous epithelium that allows it to endure friction without damage and to resist the immunological actions caused by semen and sperm. In comparison, the anus is a delicate mechanism of small muscles that comprise an "exit-only" passage. Anal intercourse is like using a highway exit ramp as an entrance ramp. That makes for problems—one of them being infection by the AIDS virus.

The Church tells us that God does not create a person with homosexual desires. According to the *Catechism* (2357), "Tradition has always declared that 'homosexual acts are intrinsically disordered.' They are contrary to the natural law. They close the sexual act to the gift of life. They do not proceed from a genuine affective and sexual complementarity. Under no circumstances can they be approved." A person may be born with a greater susceptibility to homosexuality, just as some people are born with a greater tendency toward other sins, for instance, anger. Yet in neither case does the tendency excuse giving in to sinful desires.

Is this view a self-righteous condemnation of homosexuality? Did Jesus not say, "Let those who are without sin throw the first stone"? Does the Bible not say, in Matthew 21:31, that prostitutes will enter the kingdom of heaven before the self-righteous hypocrites of the day, and could the same not be said of homosexuals? That may be true, but if prostitutes will enter heaven ahead of hypocrites, it is not because they committed prostitution, but because they changed their habits and returned to the Father. Therefore, when we cite this verse in reference to homosexuals, we have to conclude that they, too, must first repent of their sinfulness—which they may not even recognize as being sinful. To paraphrase G.K. Chesterton, as far as sin is concerned, there are two kinds of people: not those who sin and those who do not sin, but those who know that they are sinners and those who do not know that they are sinners.

We should make a distinction between homosexuality as an orientation and homosexuality as a sexual activity, as the *Catechism* (2357) does. When the Church uses the term "disorder," she does not refer to its medical sense, but to its moral sense: something "disordered" is contrary to the order of the natural law. Homosexuality as an orientation is considered an "*objective* disorder" because it is seen as "ordered toward an intrinsic moral evil," but it is not considered sinful. Homosexuality as a sexual activity is seen as a "*moral* disorder," and "homosexual acts" are considered "contrary to the natural law. They close the sexual act to the gift of life." This is where sin comes in.

Therefore, we must come to the conclusion that homosexuality as a sexual activity is not a morally permissible state of life. All human beings, including homosexuals, have to overcome lust; no one gets a pass on this task. Lust is sinful, whether it is homosexual lust or heterosexual lust. Everyone not married to a person of the opposite sex is called to celibacy. Two men or two women can certainly be friends, but not spouses; children want and need a mother and a father, not two interchangeable individuals playing "de-gendered" roles.

Anthony Esolen mentions the case of a Catholic pastor in Providence, Rhode Island, who recently fired his music director because the man had "married" another man, as was known to the people in the congregation. Esolen comments,

Had the priest not fired him, I can tell you what every teenage boy in the pews would have concluded: that the Church doesn't really believe what she says, and that when it comes to sex, you may do as you please. [...] But several people in the congregation decided to interrupt the Nicene Creed at the next Sunday Mass, singing "All Are Welcome," knowing they would be showered with praise by the people who matter, namely reporters for the local television stations and newspapers, and leaders of opinion in the best "progressive" and "inclusive" societies.

It remains true that God loves the sinner, not the sin. Therefore, homosexuals are not to be hated or accused or scorned; they are to be loved and prayed for, as we are all children of the same Father. A great strategy is that we should do all of the praying, and leave all of the judging up to God. The *Catechism* (2358) confirms this: "The number of men and women who have deep-seated homosexual tendencies is not negligible. [...] They must be accepted with respect, compassion, and sensitivity. Every sign of unjust discrimination in their regard should be avoided."

However, the gay lobby loves to play the card of "hurt feelings." They accuse Catholics, with their rigid morality, of hurting the feelings of homosexuals. The "hurt feelings" argument has been used brilliantly by liberal-progressives to silence dissenters. Sociology Professor David Carlin says about this argument, "In the old days, the Catholic Church used the Inquisition to silence Galileo, but the 'hurt feelings' device is much more effective than the Roman Inquisition ever was. At least the Inquisition gave Galileo a trial. Our liberal-progressives don't bother going through a time-wasting trial. Say something that has the odor of heresy about it, and you will be condemned instantaneously." However, morality is more than a matter of "feelings" and "beliefs." Moral "rights" and "duties" trump personal "feelings" and "beliefs," because they are objective, universal, and absolute.

Terence Cardinal Cooke of New York City saw a need for a ministry which would assist homosexual Catholics in adhering to Catholic teaching on sexual behavior. It is important to stress that he did not envision a gay-reversal therapy. Cooke invited John Harvey to New York to begin the work of *Courage International* together with the late psychologist Fr. Benedict Groeschel, a Franciscan Friar of the Renewal. The group consists of laymen and laywomen, usually under anonymous discretion, together with a priest, to encourage its members with meetings, counseling, and prayer and to help them abstain from acting on their sexual desires and to live chastely according to the Church's teachings on homosexuality. The *Catechism* (2359) again: "Homosexual persons are called to chastity. By the virtues of self-mastery that teach them inner freedom, at times by the support of disinterested friendship, by prayer and sacramental grace, they can and should gradually and resolutely approach Christian perfection."

A sacrifice it certainly is! Therefore, the *Catechism* (2358) invites homosexuals "to unite to the sacrifice of the Lord's Cross the difficulties they may encounter from their condition."

8

Euthanasia

The euthanasia debate is often tied to the question: What is a meaningful life, and can it be ended when it is no longer meaningful? Probably everyone has a different personal answer to the question of meaningfulness, but let us try to come up with an answer that is based on Catholic morality.

What Is a Meaningful Life?

Very often in life, we experience moments in which everything appears very meaningful to us. This is usually when things are going our way or are simply going "well" for us—whatever that means. Yet when suffering hits us—sickness, terminal illness, accidents, disasters, catastrophes—we struggle. How can these things happen, we wonder, if life is supposed to be so meaningful? It is certainly a life-size question that calls for a life-saving answer.

Our first problem is that afflictions are distributed *unpredictably*: they strike the just as well as the unjust, believers as well as nonbelievers, the good and the bad alike. There seems to be no pattern. We all seem to have the same chances of being stricken by evil and suffering; no one is exempt; even one's religion does not seem to make a difference. Suffering could well be called the truest democratic experience of them all.

Our second problem is that afflictions are distributed so *unequally*: some people have to stomach so much more than others. Some receive one blow after another, whereas others are apportioned meagerly. At times, we meet people who remain erect in a hurricane of misery; then again, we come across people who lament endlessly about trifles. We were created equal, but surely not as far as misery is concerned.

147

Anyone eager to build a system explaining all of this might eventually be buried under a collapsing house of cards. Nothing seems to fit, nothing seems to make sense. Yet religion is the only place where we may search for a life-saving answer. Whereas suffering may be as painful to Humanists, Marxists, and Buddhists as it is to Jews and Christians, only the latter are haunted with this piercing question: "Why has God abandoned me?" Believing in a God of love, believing in a good Creation, believing in the Providence of an all-loving God, causes the pain of suffering to penetrate to a deeper level—to the level of "Is something wrong between God and me?"

How are we to deal with all of this if life is supposed to be so meaningful? Let us acknowledge first that we do not live in a hedonistic paradise. We should ask ourselves the question: do we really admire those who appear to have a life of ease? What most of us admire, instead, are lives of courage and sacrifice. We have a high regard for people who overcome hardship, deprivation, or weakness so as to achieve some notable success; for people who stand against some great evil, or who relinquish their own pleasures to alleviate the sufferings of others. Apparently, the maximization of creaturely pleasure is not a top priority in most lives, and certainly not in the lives of Christians.

The question arises of where suffering comes from if God is an all-loving God. The Bible considers suffering a consequence of the Fall in Paradise. True, the "thorns and thistles" may have always been there, but since the Fall, they have been felt, not only as painful, but also as distressing, as something "evil." Thomas Aquinas makes a very astute remark in this context: "Some say that the animals, which are wild now and kill other animals, were not that way [in paradise…]. But this is entirely unreasonable. The nature of animals was not changed by the sin of man." Aquinas is right; after the Fall the world did not change, but we did. Without sin, physical evils would not rankle or embitter us. Only humans can get depressed. Only humans take diseases and catastrophes as something that should not be, as something that seems to be acting against them personally. Animals may "dislike" these things; they can certainly feel pain, but that would not rankle or embitter them. They do not question pain in terms of "Why me?"

Looking at things this way gives us a completely different perspective on evil and suffering. Since the Fall, we are no longer "good" people who suffer "bad" things; instead we are "bad" people who enjoy many "good" things. In other words, not only is there much good in the worst of us, but also much bad in the best of us. We should never turn misery into self-pity. As Jesus once said, "No one is good but God alone." Who is to say that suffering is all bad, or bad forever? God is certainly able to use suffering for a better purpose. There is something therapeutic about suffering—it has the potential to redeem us, transform us, and transfigure us. It is no wonder that redemption is a culmination point in the Bible. We find it already in the Jewish Scriptures, when some take upon themselves the sins and burdens of others so that all will eventually be free of the consequences of sin. This is sometimes called vicarious atonement.

This belief features strongly in the famous story about Abraham's plea for Sodom. Asking God, "Will you indeed destroy the righteous with the wicked?" Abraham starts negotiating: Suppose there are fifty righteous within the city, will you then destroy the place and not spare it for the fifty righteous who are in it? Next, Abraham whittles this further down: What about forty-five? What about forty? What about thirty? Suppose twenty are found there? At last, he gets God down to ten: "For the sake of ten I will not destroy it."

This story of Abraham has a sequel, counting further down from ten to one, when God says to the prophet Jeremiah: "Run back and forth through the streets of Jerusalem. [...] Search her squares to see if you can find a man, one who does justice and seeks the truth; that I may pardon her." Ultimately, that one man will be found in Jesus of Nazareth, the Son of Man, the Christ, the Savior. It was the High Priest Caiaphas who spoke to the Sanhedrin these prophetic words: "One man should die for the people."

There is something very peculiar going on here. We tend to ask God not to treat the just the way the unjust deserve to be treated, but, instead, God decides to treat the unjust in the same way that he treats the just—as if they were just, too. God, in fact, somehow pardons the unjust majority because of the tiny just minority. This was the "mission" of Jesus Christ—through him, and him alone, humanity would be pardoned from Sin. Jesus gave us our human dignity back, but at the cost of his own. Each time we ask God, "Why me?" we should listen carefully to hear Jesus whisper in response, "Why me?"

Christians see the story of Abraham and Isaac as a profound allegory for the sacrifice of Jesus on the Cross. Like Isaac, Jesus was a father's only beloved son. Like Isaac, Jesus carried uphill the wood for his own sacrifice. When Isaac asks, "where is the sheep for the burnt offering?" Abraham's response proved to be prophetic. Since there is no punctuation in the Hebrew original, verse 8 of Genesis 22 could be read as follows: "God will provide Himself, the Lamb, for a burnt offering"—the Lamb being Jesus Christ, God himself. The Cross is not mere darkness, since it is also part of God's Providence. The ancient Church used to sing, "God reigns from the wood of the Cross." In other words, suffering is not meant to make us bitter, but *better*. To the left of Jesus's Cross was someone who felt bitter, to the right someone who felt better. We may choose who we want to be!

Are we glorifying suffering here? Not really. But it must be said that we live in a world that runs away from suffering; just look at our bathroom cabinets filled with painkillers. Since the time of our youth, we have been conditioned to view suffering as an impediment to happiness. This worldview, which is embedded in our culture, tells us that the less we suffer, the happier we will be. Yet we could be missing out on another dimension of suffering, for suffering has the mysterious potential of redeeming us, transforming us, transfiguring us. Although we feel that the less we suffer, the closer to God we will be, the opposite may be true. Whereas Stoics say "Suffering is nothing," Christians say "Suffering is everything." In everything that happens, even in suffering, we can discern God's "hand"—not a hand that causes all of the good and bad things that we read about in the newspapers, but a hand that holds all of these things together by saving them for a better purpose. It is in such a "hand" that God holds the future of each one of us. We do not know what the future holds, but we do know who holds the future.

What is the conclusion of all of this? Life is always meaningful, in good times and in bad times, in joy and in suffering. In his first homily as pontiff, in 2005, Pope Benedict XVI insisted: "We are not some casual and meaningless product of evolution. Each of us is the result of a thought of God. Each of us is willed, each of us is loved, each of us is necessary." This is a life-long significance that never ends, continuing even after death. This tells us that there is no moment in life when we should actively end life. Because the value of each individual life is intrinsic, there is no moment in human life when that value ceases to exist.

This does not change the fact that many people have died or will die without ever having been welcomed into life, without ever having received love, comfort, or even justice. Some of us experience lots of rejection, violence, poverty, suffering, pain, and injustice. Some of us may not have much to live for. This is a reality that calls for a Last Judgment, as mentioned in the Bible. As a matter of fact, a final judgment is the answer to many questions we may have in life. What about all those people who have experienced so little joy in their lives, or who were given the "wrong genes"? What about all those victims of infertility, abortion, eugenics, and euthanasia? What about all those people who cannot be called back to life to receive a bit more warmth and love here? What about those neglected by their spouses, their parents, or their children? So many people had hoped for something good but received so much evil and suffering instead. What are we to do with all of these people?

Put differently, there are many "debit" accounts that still need to be settled—not so much those little accounts that one might like to settle with one's neighbors, but rather those enormous accounts that caused sorrow, affliction, and disaster to millions of people. The fact that we speak in terms of "accounts that need to be settled" implies already that we can go up "into Heaven" to see everything dimly from God's perspective. This is where the idea of a "final judgment" comes from; if there were no final judgment, those accounts would remain unsettled. In a God-less world, in a world without purposes, there is no hope that those issues would ever be addressed. Yet, the earth is crying out for justice! It makes for an ever-meaningful life, even beyond death.

Because we are free human beings with morality, we will be held accountable for our choices in life. Evil is a matter of bad choices, and bad choices affect not only our own lives, but also those of others. That is what a final judgment is about. If there is no instant repayment for good or bad actions and choices, there must be a final repayment in the final-final stage of life. We need and deserve to be judged, if God is also a Just God. Good actions God can reward with Heaven, bad ones with Hell. As St. Augustine put it, God "did not will to save us without us." God does not judge us on our feelings and emotions, for those are sometimes beyond our control, but he does judge us on our free choices in life. Did we follow our moral compass? That is the vital question.

From this, it follows conclusively that the ultimate consequence of human freedom is the existence of an eternal Heaven as well as an eternal Hell. Certainly no sane person wants Hell to exist, just as no sane person wants evil to exist; but evil does exist. If there is a free will, then there must be evil; if evil and eternity exist, then there must be Hell. Hell is only evil eternalized. C.S. Lewis called Hell "the greatest monument to human freedom." The *Catechism* (1861) puts it this way: "Our freedom has the power to make choices for ever, with no turning back."

What, then, of God's forgiveness? It exists also, but not unconditionally. Pope Benedict XVI put it this way: Unconditional forgiveness—the abolition of Hell—would be a kind of "cheap grace," to which the German Protestant theologian Dietrich Bonhoeffer rightly objected in the face of the appalling evil that he encountered in Nazi Germany in his day. If God does not will to save us without us, then there must be not only salvation, but also damnation. If there is eternal salvation, there must also be eternal damnation. We cannot blame God for this, because people who commit grave evil condemn themselves. Hell is a state of "definitive self-exclusion from communion with God," says the *Catechism* (1033). The afterlife would be a period of repayment—for the good things done as well as the bad things done. As C.S. Lewis put it, those "who did most for the present world were just those who thought most of the next."

Fortunately, says the Catholic Church, there is also something in between Heaven and Hell, a kind of "middle state" called Purgatory. As Fr. Benedict Groeschel put it, "Purgatory is not a temporary hell, but a preliminary heaven." It is a place or state where human imperfection is corrected in the "fire of purification" before we can enter

God's Heaven where "nothing unclean shall enter" (Rev. 21:27). This is counter to the cheap optimism that prevails nowadays in the minds of many, holding that the life of practically everybody automatically ends up in a state of bliss. True, there is also God's infinite mercy. But mercy does not wipe out all evil, only the evil that we ask forgiveness for. God's mercy is boundless, but to access it requires repentance. "Lord, have mercy" does not translate into "God, go easy on me." Mercy does not mean to be "soft on crime." God's mercy and His justice go hand in hand. St. Augustine advises us, "After sin, hope for mercy; before sin, fear justice."

Where does euthanasia belong in this discussion? Some promote euthanasia because they believe that there is nothing beyond death. Others toy with euthanasia, believing that everyone will end up in a state of bliss no matter what they have done. Others decide on euthanasia because they want to be in charge of their own final judgment. What all these people have in common is that they do not believe that there is a Last Judgement after death. The Catholic Church will tell them that because of God's Last Judgment, they should not craft their own "last" judgment, but leave that decision up to God. Euthanasia is not something for us to decide on our own.

Prolonging Life

At this point in time, the power of medical technology is greater than ever before. Decades ago, doctors made full use of the little bit they happened to know to prevent us from dying. Nowadays, doctors use everything that they have come to know to keep us alive. They are able to relieve pain with medication, to treat our cancers, to artificially feed us, to connect us to a ventilator, and to resuscitate us. How are we to deal with these overpowering advancements in medical technology?

It is obvious that prolonging life is a good thing, and that doctors ought to do everything possible to keep us alive. But are there also situations where it is permissible to *not* prolong life any further? Not prolonging life is sometimes called passive or indirect euthanasia. Whereas euthanasia in general is the practice of intentionally ending human life, passive euthanasia occurs when the patient dies because the medical professionals either omit something necessary to keep the patient alive or withdraw something that is keeping the patient alive. Does this not mean that we are taking life and death decisions into our own hands? How should we assess this in moral terms?

The first question that we should ask is this: Are we at the mercy of medical technology? The answer is a cautious No. The Church does not oblige Catholics to accept medical treatment near the end of life to prolong life and delay death. Since the Middle Ages, Catholic theologians have recognized that human beings are not morally obligated to undergo every possible medical treatment to save their lives. Prolonging life is not always a moral duty. Treatments that are beyond the economic means of the person, or which only prolong the suffering of a dying person, or are unduly burdensome or sorrowful to a particular patient, such as amputation or painful chemotherapy, may not be morally obligatory in a particular case. When death is imminent, one may refuse forms of treatment that would only result in a precarious and burdensome prolongation of life. An instruction not to provide such treatment, when communicated ahead of time to family and friends, may give great comfort to loved ones during emotionally stressful times.

The Church knows very well about the overpowering power of medical technology. The *Catechism* (2278) is very explicit on this:

> Discontinuing medical procedures that are burdensome, dangerous, extraordinary, or disproportionate to the expected outcome can be legitimate; it is the refusal of "over-zealous" treatment. Here one does not will to cause death; one's inability to impede it is merely accepted. The decisions should be made by the patient if he is competent and able or, if not, by those legally entitled to act for the patient, whose reasonable will and legitimate interests must always be respected.

The second question to address is that of providing pain relief to near-death patients or terminally ill patients. This is known as palliative care—medical care for patients with terminal illness in need of pain relief by administration of opioid drugs. Physicians and researchers have insisted, repeatedly, that it is a myth that opioids administered for pain relief can be expected to hasten death. This indicates that there is nothing morally wrong with administering pain relief, for it is not even a form of passive euthanasia.

The situation will be different if or when it is proven that opioid drugs do, in fact, hasten death. Even then, administering pain relief might be morally permissible if the main intention is to relieve the pain, not to intentionally cause the death. In other words, providing necessary pain relief, even if it shortens life, is not active euthanasia unless the explicit intent is to kill. The *Catechism* (2279) is very clear on this:

> The use of painkillers to alleviate the sufferings of the dying, even at the risk of shortening their days, can be morally in conformity with human dignity if death is not willed as either an end or a means, but only foreseen and tolerated as inevitable. Palliative care is a special form of disinterested charity. As such it should be encouraged.

This moral assessment is based on the Principle of Double Effect. It is morally permissible to perform an act that has both a good effect and a bad effect if all of the following conditions are met: (1) The act to be done must be good in itself or at least indifferent. (2) The good effect must not be obtained by means of the bad effect. (3) The bad effect must not be intended for itself, but only permitted. (4) There must be a proportionately grave reason for permitting the bad effect.

Based on these conditions, giving pain relief treatment is morally justified, provided it is given with the primary intention to relieve pain, and excuses any unavoidable, but unwanted, life-shortening effect of doing so. The principle makes intention in the mind of the doctor a crucial factor in judging the moral correctness of the doctor's action. Providing necessary pain relief, even if it shortens life, is a form of "passive" euthanasia and fulfills all of the conditions of the Principle of Double Effect; "active" euthanasia, on the other hand, fulfills none of them. It would be morally wrong to hasten death intentionally in order to cut short the suffering of a terminally ill patient.

One word of caution, however. Canadian McGill Professor Margaret A. Somerville makes an important distinction between relieving pain and relieving suffering. She says, "Saying that patients must be offered all treatment necessary to relieve their *pain*, even if that treatment could or would shorten life, or they must be offered all treatment necessary to relieve their *suffering*, may seem the same. But, properly interpreted, the former statement does not open up the possibility of legitimating euthanasia; the latter could do so and could affect the law accordingly." There is an important distinction here. In cases of terminal cancer or some other painful illness, the doctor gradually increases the dosage of pain relief over a period of weeks, or even months, to relieve *pain*. Since these patients build up a tolerance to the drug, they usually do not lose consciousness until they are near the point of death. However, this is different from a patient being given a large dose of morphine without having been able to build up a tolerance. Some doctors use the deliberate sedation of patients to deep unconsciousness for the purpose of relieving *suffering*. This is called Terminal Sedation (TS).

The Catholic Bioethics Center advises us not to use the expression "quality of life" in this context, because it is used by advocates of "active" euthanasia to suggest that some lives are not worth living and have lost their "quality." As the Center puts it, "While illness and other circumstances can make life very difficult, they cannot diminish the inestimable worth of each human life created by God." Life itself is always a good, and is a quality that can never be lost or diminish. Still, we need not cling to this life at all costs, since the life to which we have been called in Christ is incomparably better.

A third question to address is that of stopping artificial nutrition and hydration of a near-death patient. When this is done to allow patients to die from an underlying condition, rather than to unnecessarily prolonging their suffering, it may be morally justified. For example, in the last hours, even days, of a cancer patient's life, or if a sick person's body is no longer able to process food and water, there is no moral obligation to provide nutrition and hydration any longer. These patients will die of their disease or of organ failure before starvation or dehydration can kill them.

On the other hand, when the withdrawal of nutrition and hydration is intended to kill the person or will be the immediate and direct cause of doing so, apart from any disease or failure of their bodies, to withdraw food and water is an act of active euthanasia, a grave sin against the natural law and the law of God. The case of Terri Schiavo is a famous example of such an error; while there was some disagreement as to her exact medical condition, she was not dying. Indeed, when other artificial means of support were withdrawn, she continued to live, so that the withdrawal of her food and water directly caused her death. This is considered morally unacceptable in the eyes of the Catholic Church.

Pope Benedict XVI made this very clear in his 2004 address to physicians:

> The evaluation of probabilities, founded on waning hopes for recovery when the vegetative state is prolonged beyond a year, cannot ethically justify the cessation or interruption of minimal care for the patient, including nutrition and hydration. Death by starvation or dehydration is, in fact, the only possible outcome as a result of their withdrawal. In this sense it ends up becoming, if done knowingly and willingly, true and proper euthanasia by omission.

In summary, nutrition and hydration, like bathing and changing the patient's position to avoid bedsores, is a matter of ordinary care that is owed to the patient. This is true even if nutrition and hydration are delivered artificially, as when a baby is bottle-fed or a sick person is tube-fed. Nutrition and hydration may only be discontinued when they cannot achieve their natural purposes, such as when the body can no longer process them, or when during the death process they would only prolong the person's suffering. In such a case, the patient dies of the underlying disease. On the other hand, if starvation and dehydration is the foreseeable cause of death, to withhold or withdrawn nutrition and hydration is gravely immoral.

Behind all these moral considerations is the Catholic proclamation of the sanctity of life. According to divine law (the Bible), we are created in God's image and knit together by God in the womb: "For you formed my inward parts; you wove me in my mother's womb" (Psalm 139:13). Therefore, no one should ever choose to end their own life or be killed against their will. We should always try to prolong life, unless there are strong reasons not to do so any longer.

Shortening Life

Whereas administering pain relief treatment or refusing further prolongation of burdensome medical treatment may be permissible forms of passive or indirect euthanasia, the situation is different with regard to acts of shortening life, usually called active or direct euthanasia. This latter form of euthanasia has been defined by Pope John Paul II, in his encyclical *Evangelium Vitae*, as "an action or omission which of itself and by intention causes death, with the purpose of eliminating all suffering." As representative of Christ on earth, the Holy Father holds that "euthanasia is a grave violation of the law of God, since it is the deliberate and morally unacceptable killing of a human person." This amounts to murder, in spite of the fact that killing, not only at the beginning but also at the end of life, has become legal and has even been championed in more and more countries.

The prefix "eu-" in euthanasia means "good," but euthanasia is certainly not "good" by definition. Active euthanasia is, in fact, a fundamentally unreasonable act, because in Catholic morality, the value of each individual life is intrinsic. As the *Catechism* (2324) puts it, "Intentional euthanasia, whatever its forms or motives, is murder. It is gravely contrary to the dignity of the human person and to the respect due to the living God, his Creator." The value of a life does not depend upon what a person is physically able to do, experience, or achieve. The life of a comatose person, or of a terminally ill patient, has the same dignity and worth as the life of a fully functioning adult. The proper rule, as Robert P. George of Princeton University puts it, should be, "Always to care, never to kill."

Supporters of euthanasia often justify active euthanasia, or physician-assisted suicide, on the grounds that the pain of terminal illness is too great for the average person to bear. They hold that it is more merciful to kill suffering patients than to keep them alive. They cleverly swap one moral value, the sanctity of life, with another moral value, the prevention of suffering. They use the euphemism of "mercy killing," and defend it with a reference to a person's "right to die"—although there is no right to die, because there is no duty to die.

Those who truly provide "aid in dying" at the end-stage of life are hospice workers, hospital chaplains, nurses, counselors, psychologists, and concerned relatives—but not those doctors who provide lethal drugs to people who are usually not even their own patients. For doctors to administer means of death is a disgrace to the medical profession and a sign of disrespect for the final stage of life's journey. All of us, including doctors, have the moral duty to improve quality of life, even at the end of life, and patients have the right to receive this care. Passionate doctors should end the patient's *pain*, not the patient's *life*. When they decide otherwise, they make all people involved accomplices in a murder—pharmacists, nurses, family members, friends, and even society itself.

Similar to the shift in terms that characterized the abortion debate, arguments and terms supporting euthanasia have shifted from "pain relief" to "mercy-killing," then to "assisted suicide," and finally to "autonomy" and "self-determination"—which means that all people should be allowed to decide for themselves when and whether they want to end their lives, without any interference from churches, governments, or any other entity. This was probably a rhetorical and strategic shift, but it ended up undermining its own logic when it came to legalization of doctor-assisted suicide, because "legalization" requires, per definition, the involvement of at least the government and medical professionals—elements that can only hamper any personal and individual autonomy. It is ironic that the will of the individual has become the authoritative principle in this discussion, just as the will of the state was the deciding authority for euthanasia in Nazi Germany. Now it is the individual, not the state, who orders the killing of "useless" people.

It should not be surprising, then, that once assisted suicide had been legalized in the Netherlands in the name of autonomy, there was no longer any way to argue for limitations on its use. This opened the door for active euthanasia, even in its non-voluntary and involuntary forms. Once we adopt the principle that suicide is acceptable, or even "good," the fences that legislators may try to erect around it inevitably become arbitrary. In Belgium, nowadays, even children are accepted as subjects for euthanasia. How much lower can the "Low Countries" of Belgium and the Netherlands sink?

Dr. Theo de Boer, who reviewed nearly four thousand cases of assisted suicide on behalf of the Ministry of Health and the Ministry of Justice in the Netherlands, became gradually more troubled by what he was seeing. He discovered that the number of cases in 2014 was nearly three times the number indicated by the 2002 figures. Initially, 95% of the patients had a terminal disease, but gradually more and more cases of dementia, psychiatric illnesses, and age-related complaints were included. Current Dutch law allows minors aged 12 to 15 to choose euthanasia with parental permission; after age 16, young people can make the decisions with only parental involvement. What we clearly see here is a society that is sliding down the proverbial slippery slope.

Active euthanasia has often been euphemistically called "doctor-assisted suicide." Expressed in such terms, it sounds reasonable, but what exactly is reasonable about self-destruction? Euthanasia is based on the assumption that certain people will be better served by being dead—a dubious premise indeed, as Cardinal Seán O'Malley rightly put it. Not only is the term "doctor-assisted suicide" confusing—for how can it be suicide if it is assisted?—but it is also misleading, as the only "assistance" the patient receives from the doctor is a prescription to be filled at a pharmacy.

Therefore, a more realistic and accurate description of "doctor-assisted suicide" would be "doctor-prescribed death." In this context, one might argue that doctors should rather be guided by their centuries-old Hippocratic Oath: "I will not give a lethal drug to anyone if I am asked, nor will I advise such a plan." We should ask ourselves the question of how we can trust a health care system in which medical doctors save some lives but end others. The McGill University Professor Margaret Somerville is right when she says, "Doctors' absolute repugnance to killing people is necessary to maintaining people's and society's trust in them."

Medical doctors have become more involved as accomplices in euthanasia than they could ever have imagined. The *Affordable Care Act* of US President Barack Obama has been charged with creating bureaucratic "death panels" that would ration health care, effectively deciding in some cases who lives and who dies. This could mean that grandma or grandpa could be rejected for medical treatment when they get sick. Indeed, Steven Rattner, former counselor to the Treasury secretary in the Obama administration, wrote in the *New York Times* in 2012, "We need death panels." In 2014, Dr. Ezekiel Emanuel, who helped craft Obamacare as health-policy adviser at the White House's Office of Management and Budget, said he thought people should die at the age of 75.[1] More and more people seem to think death panels, intended to reduce the costs of treating people who get sick but do not die soon enough, might not be such a bad idea, after all. Rationing of care is coming, perhaps even soon. While this may not be euthanasia in its strict sense, it would cut some people off from further medical care, thus shortening their time to live.

As said earlier, changing terminology does not change the reality it refers to. "Aid in dying" for terminally ill patients is a seductive and misleading term for "aid in suicide." Proponents of this kind of "aid" often deliberately avoid the word "suicide" to mask reality, and they tend to use the term "terminally ill" instead. However, not only is the *diagnosis* that doctors make about a terminal illness sometimes off, but very often their *prognosis* is too. Any prediction of how many months someone has to live is at best an educated guess, certainly not a scientific assessment—and even if it were scientific, science has occasionally proven to be wrong. No one should make life-and-death decisions based on someone's best guess. Words such as "mercy," "dignity," and "compassion" cannot alter the fact that "mercy-killing" is a form of killing—and, when done to oneself, it is a form of self-destruction or suicide.

As discussed earlier, moral rights and moral duties go hand in hand—if there are no duties, then there are no rights. When it comes to euthanasia, there is no duty to die, so there is no right to die. As always, once we uncouple rights from duties, new "rights" pop up like mushrooms, one of which is the newly invented "last civil right" to die. These bogus new rights are invented and claimed on the spot, but the question of duty is utterly lost. At best they can become entitlements, enforced by a so-called legal system, the laws of the land. But the law of the land is not always a reflection of the moral law. The *Catechism* (2277) concludes:

---

1. Read more at http://www.wnd.com/2016/01/death-panels-resurrected-under-new-medicare-rules/#1Hwrod dYSGwgOBoS.99.

Whatever its motives and means, direct euthanasia consists in putting an end to the lives of handicapped, sick, or dying persons. It is morally unacceptable. Thus an act or omission which, of itself or by intention, causes death in order to eliminate suffering constitutes a murder gravely contrary to the dignity of the human person and to the respect due to the living God, his Creator.

There is never a moment in life when life is no longer meaningful. The compassion we show to the dying is not earned by things they accomplished in life, any more than it should be earned by the things an unborn baby might one day achieve. You cannot earn or forfeit your humanity; human descent is enough to merit human rights, both in living and in dying. There are rights that we should claim as human beings, and there are duties which we owe others as human beings. No one has the right to take those God-given rights away.

How Dead Is Brain-Dead?

Before the development of modern medical care, the diagnosis of death was relatively straightforward. Patients were "dead" when they were cold, blue, and stiff with *rigor mortis*. More recently, this was followed by a more scientific diagnosis, called *clinical death*. It is the medical term for cessation of blood circulation and breathing, the two necessary criteria to sustain biological life. Clinical death occurs when the heart stops beating in a regular rhythm, a condition called cardiac arrest. When your heart stops, your brain no longer gets the blood it needs to function, and you lose consciousness immediately—unless the heartbeat and circulation can be restored by cardiac massage within a few minutes. Prior to the invention, in the second half of the 20th century, of cardiopulmonary resuscitation (CPR), defibrillation, epinephrine injection, and other treatments, the absence of blood circulation and breathing was historically considered to be the official definition of death.

At the onset of clinical death, consciousness is not lost until 15 to 20 seconds later. Measurable brain activity stops within 20 to 40 seconds. Although most tissues and organs of the body can survive clinical-death for considerable periods of time, the brain cannot.

Without special treatment after circulation is restarted, full recovery of the brain is exceptional when more than five minutes of clinical-death at normal body temperature have occurred. Brain injury is therefore the limiting factor for recovery from clinical-death. However, reducing body temperature by 3° Celsius after restarting blood circulation could double the time window of recovery from clinical death from five to ten minutes without brain damage. This induced hypothermia technique is becoming more common in emergency medicine.

With the increasing ability of the medical community to resuscitate people who have no respiration, heartbeat, or other external signs of life, the need for a better definition of death became pertinent. This need gained even greater urgency with a rising demand for organ transplantation. The law requires that the donor of a vital organ be dead before the organ can be removed. This is known as the "dead donor law," but with a standard definition of cardiac death, heart transplants are not easily possible.

In 1968, an ad-hoc committee at Harvard Medical School published a pivotal report to define irreversible coma. The Harvard criteria gradually gained consensus towards what is now known as *brain-death*. A brain-dead individual has no clinical evidence of brain function, which includes no response to pain and no cranial nerve reflexes—that is, no pupillary response (fixed pupils), no corneal reflexes, no oculo-vestibular reflex, no gag reflex, and no spontaneous respirations. When removed from the ventilator, the active brain will cause the patient to breathe spontaneously—due to a rise of the CO_2 level in the blood—whereas a dead brain would give no response.

The medical profession initially was eager to accept the notion of brain-death because of the rapidly increasing use of ventilators, with some patients becoming permanently "ventilator-dependent." In the words of philosopher Michael Hanby, "There was no need to establish precise criteria for determining death within an instant of its occurring until it became technologically possible to hold people in a kind of limbo and to harvest their organs for transplant."

When the patient has a dead brain as well as a dead brain stem, there may still be spinal cord reflexes that can be induced (a knee jerk, for example). In some brain-dead patients, when the hand or foot is touched in a particular manner, the touch will still cause a short reflex movement. So in addition to the aforementioned clinical signs of brain death, many physicians and most state laws require other, confirmatory tests before declaring a patient brain-dead. The two most common are the electroencephalogram (EEG) and the cerebral-blood-flow (CBF) test. The EEG measures brain voltage in microvolts. It is so sensitive that the static electricity in a person's clothes will give a squiggle on the EEG (a false positive), but all real positive responses suggest the brain is still functioning. The CBF test involves the injection of a mild radioactive isotope into the blood stream. By placing a radioactivity counter over the head, one can measure the amount of blood flow into the brain. If there is no blood flow to the brain during this test, the brain is considered dead.

It is important, though, to distinguish between brain-death and states that may mimic brain-death—such as barbiturate overdose, alcohol intoxication, sedative overdose, hypothermia, hypoglycemia, coma, or chronic vegetative states. Some comatose patients can still recover, and some patients with severe irreversible neurological dysfunction will nonetheless retain some lower brain functions such as spontaneous respiration, although both cortex and brain stem no longer function. We should mention also that patients who suffer brain-death are not in coma; patients in coma may or may not progress to brain-death. Then there are patients who are in what is called a "vegetative state"; they have far more lower-brain function, and a bit more upper brain-stem function, than a patient in deep coma. In either case, however, the patient is considered alive, because he or she still has some neurological signs.

All of this raises the question of why the brain is considered more important than the heart when it comes to death. The brain controls all our bodily functions, but there are two things it cannot do. Firstly, the brain cannot store oxygen, so it is affected by a lack of oxygen after just a few seconds. Secondly, the brain cannot store glucose, so it starves in a very short time. These two conditions require a heartbeat to deliver oxygen and glucose, so when there is a cardiac arrest, resuscitation must be done within five minutes, or the body's main control center breaks down permanently. The heart can still continue to beat without brain activity—normally, the heart beats without nervous control, but the brain can alter its rate—yet all other processes in the body will gradually come to a halt when they are no longer controlled by the brain. When the brain dies, all the body's organs will eventually and inevitably collapse.

Although electrical activity of the brain can stop completely, or drop to such a low level that it cannot be detected with most equipment, the lack of electrical activity—a flat-EEG—would not be decisive, because it sometimes also occurs during deep anesthesia or cardiac arrest. In the United States, a flat-EEG test is not required to certify death, but it is considered to have confirmatory value. Once brain-death has been confirmed, we speak of "legal death," even if the heart is still beating and mechanical ventilation can keep other vital organs completely alive and functional. Patients in this state have presumably died, even though ventilators can continue to oxygenate their bodies and preserve organs for a limited period of time.

This brings us to this other reason why brain-death is considered a better criterion for death than clinical death: the growing need for organ transplants. Although some deny that there is a connection between the push for brain-death proof and the need for organ transplants, even the 1968 Harvard report explicitly mentions this connection, offering two reasons for its approach. First, advances in medicine were allowing brain-damaged patients to survive for extended periods on cardiac life-support systems. Secondly—and here is the kicker—the report argued that "obsolete" criteria for the determination of death were aggravating the shortage of organs available for transplant. Brain-dead patients possess vital organs that are in good condition, because their hearts are still beating. Now these patients may be used as a source for transplantable organs.

We are on a slippery slope that led to the "innovation," in the 1990s, of "Donation after Cardiac Death" (DCD). A donor-after-DCD is a donor who has suffered devastating and irreversible brain injury and may be near death, but does not meet formal brain-death criteria. In these cases, it is the family who has decided to withdraw any further care. When the patient's heart stops beating, the organs are recovered in the operating room. Organs recovered from a donor-after-DCD do have some degree of oxygen deprivation during the time after the heart stops beating, but their organs are still usable (although kidneys from this type of donor may be "slow to start").

It should not come as a surprise that linking brain-death to organ transplants could potentially create moral problems. A small but growing number of ethicists warn us for what they deem an overly quick rush to procure organs for transplant—a rush which, they argue, is sometimes so hasty that "brain-dead" patients are in fact still alive when they are put to the knife. As a matter of fact, family members frequently report being placed under heavy pressure to consent to organ "harvesting."

This certainly calls for a moral assessment. What is the Church's position on this? On the one hand, the Church continues to recognize the generous nature of freely-chosen organ donation—an act that Pope John Paul II once called "particularly praiseworthy" for offering "a chance of health and even of life itself to the sick who sometimes have no other hope." The *Catechism* (2296) reinforces this: "Organ donation after death is a noble and meritorious act and is to be encouraged as an expression of generous solidarity." Key here, however, are the words "after death." On the other hand, Pope John Paul II said in his encyclical *Evangelium Vitae* (15) that serious and real forms of active euthanasia "could occur for example when, in order to increase the availability of organs for transplants, organs are removed without respecting objective and adequate criteria which verify the death of the donor."

It is not only the "rush" to procure organs for transplant that has started a debate on the moral validity of the brain-death criterion. Even the criterion itself has come under attack: How dead is brain-dead? Defining death is no mere academic exercise—at least not if one accepts that one must be dead in order to be cut open and have organs taken from one's body. It is a very serious, practical, and moral issue of life and death. Dr. Robert Truog, for instance, who is an associate professor of anesthesiology at Harvard Medical School, claims that brain-dead patients are not really dead, and recommends a return to the traditional definition of death, clinical death, based on cessation of respiration and circulation rather than neurological criteria. Since there can be no certainty about the vital status of patients with total brain failure, only traditional signs—namely, irreversible cessation of heart and lung function—should be used to declare a patient dead, in his opinion.

One of the arguments in favor of such criticism is that when there is ventilator support, the bodies of brain-dead patients have been shown to undergo respiration at the cellular level through the exchange of O_2 and CO_2; they assimilate nutrients through the coordinated activity of the digestive and circulatory systems; they also fight infection and foreign bodies. If these are not symptoms of a living person, what is? Experts such as pediatrician and neonatologist Dr. Paul Byrne, MD have argued that the acceptance of brain-death confuses prognosis with diagnosis. The word "irreversible," frequently invoked in discussions of brain-death, is based on prognosis. Yet the simple fact that patients are irreversibly comatose, and *will* in all likelihood be dead shortly, does not justify the conclusion that they *are* already dead in terms of diagnosis. The prognosis of an impending death cannot be used as a diagnosis of actual death.

Needless to say, this view has its dissenters as well. James M. DuBois, professor of health care ethics at Saint Louis University, for instance, maintains that a mature human body that is functionally "decapitated," in his own words, is no longer a living human being. The fact that many parts of the body may survive and function for a time is wholly compatible with death of the human person, he says, as this is precisely what makes organ transplantation possible. His reasoning is as follows: The human heart may beat outside of the human body in a bucket of ice, and may even be transplanted and made to function again inside another human being—but still, its donor is dead. Obviously, this view would legitimize the link between brain-death and organ donation. But it is also true that a heart outside the body is no longer part of the unity of a human person until it is transplanted. The same might be said about an artificial heart.

Then there is criticism of the brain-death concept coming from an entirely different angle—from some Catholic ethicists, philosophers, and theologians. Their first line of attack is that the Church does not and cannot "define" death—at least not in a clinical sense—because that is not the Church's authority. It is the task of doctors, not the Magisterium, to determine when death has clinically occurred. The Church cannot legitimize such scientific criteria, but may at best accept them for the time being. Therefore, "brain-death" cannot be an official Church teaching. Roman Pontiffs have frequently expressed confidence in the ability of doctors to distinguish between life and death, but they cannot officially endorse the specific clinical criteria doctors have come up with—that is beyond the Church's competence. Never in history did the Church claim the authority to officially sanction a specific scientific theory—whether it is heliocentrism, evolutionary theory, or the Big Bang theory. That is science's territory. Science can be and will be revised, but dogma cannot.

This has led some Catholic thinkers to a completely different approach regarding the brain-death issue. Honesty and fairness compel us to mention this part of the discussion, although it may cause some confusion among the faithful. But at least it will make them more careful before they rush into organ donation, as organ donation is an optional charitable act, but not a moral duty. Whereas it is not the Church's job to establish clinical criteria for death, it is not the doctor's job to pinpoint the location of the human soul vs. brain. According to the *Catechism* (1005), death occurs when "the soul is separated from the body." In defining brain-death, medicine has now in effect identified the human soul with the human brain vs. soul. This is basically a materialist position. From this viewpoint, it follows that if the brain is "dead," then what is left is merely a collection of organs, no longer a human person with a soul. But it is hard, if not impossible, to identify the human soul with the human brain.

There are many reasons why the soul cannot be identical to the brain. Here are just a few. The brain is a material entity, but the mind is an immaterial, spiritual entity. The brain is governed by laws of physics, chemistry, and biology, but thoughts and beliefs in the mind are not. Whereas the brain as a material entity has characteristics such as length, width, height, and weight, the mind does not have any of those; thoughts are true or false, right or wrong, but never tall or short, heavy or light—they have no mass, size, or color.

In order to evaluate the outcome of neural states as true or false, we need something that is not neural but mental. Even if certain neural regions light up on an fMRI during certain mental activities, those lit-up state may not be causing certain mental states, but just reflecting them—correlation is not always causation.

There is another reason why the brain cannot be identical to the mind. Thinking that the brain is the principle agent of thought is as dubious as thinking that the hand is the principle agent of grasping, as opposed to a mere tool used by a human being. The mind needs the brain to function properly—that's why an intoxicated brain hampers the mind—but the brain also needs the soul and its mind to function fully. Then there are those who think that our understanding of the world—a mental activity—is done by the brain through purely neural activities. The philosopher Michael Augros uses the following analogy: You cannot count what you are seeing without using your eyes, but that does not mean your eyes are doing the counting. Similarly, while it is clear that we cannot understand anything without using our brains, it does not follow that our brains are doing the understanding. As Stephen Barr pithily puts it, "The brain does not infer the existence of the mind, the mind infers the existence of the brain." To claim that mental concepts are strictly neural events makes for a vicious circle: the very idea that concepts are nothing but neurons firing is itself nothing but neurons firing.

All these reasons, and many others, make it hard to equate the soul and its mind to the body and its brain. If indeed the soul is not the same as the body, and the mind is not the same as the brain, then brain-death may not be the best indicator of death for a human person. Is a brain-dead person necessarily a corpse without a soul? E. Christian Brugger, a Senior Fellow of Ethics at the Culture of Life Foundation, expresses "a reasonable doubt that excludes 'moral certitude' that ventilator-sustained brain dead bodies are corpses." Corpses do not have a soul, but bodies do. In this context, Brugger quotes Pope John Paul II, who told a congress on organ transplants that death is "a single event consisting in the total disintegration of that unity and integrated whole that is the personal self." Seen in this light, living human beings may derive their bodily unity, not from a central coordinating organ like the brain, but, in his own words, from the "mutual interaction among all the parts of the body." To use an analogy, a city damaged by an earthquake may still have a functional transportation system, although the communication system of phones, etc., is broken.

Alfonso Gomez-Lobo, a Catholic professor of moral philosophy at Georgetown University, gives us good reason to think that such coordination and integration cannot be linked to a single organ like the brain or spinal cord, but instead should be seen as a product of the dynamism of the organism holistically considered. Indeed, he makes the powerful point that "during the early embryonic stages of an organism, there is certainly integrated functioning of subsystems, and this happens before the brain is formed." Apparently, integration is not exclusively a neural issue. If the human organism can self-integrate and coordinate without a brain at one stage of development, this fact at least opens up the theoretical possibility that it can do so at other stages as well, even at the end stage.

Considerations such as these have also reached some Church officials. In 1997, the Archbishop of Cologne, Cardinal Joachim Meisner, issued a strong statement of opposition to the brain-death approach, responding to public debate in Germany on the subject: "The identification of brain death with the death of the human being is from a Christian viewpoint, at the present stand of the debate, no longer defensible. A human being cannot any longer be reduced to his brain function. Therefore it can neither be said that brain death is death, nor that it is a sign of death." Put differently, the mystery of how body and soul are united exceeds just brain function. While the brain does serve to "fine-tune" the body's organic unity, the source of this unity is not found in the body and its brain, but in the soul and its mind.

In an article written in 2001, Bishop Bruskewitz of Lincoln, Nebraska, and Bishop Vasa of Santa Rosa, California, along with several others, quoted the neurologist Dr. Tad Seifert, who also uses the argument that the human brain develops gradually during the first embryological stages:

> During the first six weeks of pregnancy our body lives without a brain and hence our human life does not begin with the human

brain. Certainly, the embryo is alive but his life is not bound to the functioning of his brain. Therefore, the thesis of brain death being the actual death of the person which ties human life inseparably to a functioning brain goes against this biological fact: the development of the embryonic body proves that the brain cannot be simply the seat of the human person's life or soul.

There may be another reason why we should not too easily focus on neurological criteria alone: the so-called "near-death experience" (NDE). This phenomenon refers to a broad range of personal experiences associated with impending death, encompassing sensations such as detachment from the body, feelings of levitation, total serenity, security, warmth, the experience of absolute dissolution, and the presence of a bright light. These are phenomena usually reported after an individual was very close to death—hence the term "near-death experience." According to a recent Gallup poll, approximately eight million Americans claim to have had a near-death experience; however, the exact number of people who had near-death experiences may be much higher, because people who have had such an experience may not feel comfortable discussing their experience with others, especially when such an experience is often understood as a paranormal, if not creepy, incident.

One of the first clinical studies of near-death experiences (NDEs) in cardiac arrest patients was done in 2001 by Pim van Lommel, a cardiologist in the Netherlands. With his team, he studied a group of Dutch patients who had been brain-dead from cardiac arrest but were successfully revived. Of the 344 patients who were successfully resuscitated after suffering cardiac arrest, 62 experienced "classic" NDEs, which included out-of-body experiences. The patients remembered details of their conditions during their cardiac arrest despite being clinically dead with flat-lined brain stem activity. Van Lommel concluded that his findings supported the theory that consciousness had continued despite lack of neuronal activity in the brain. What such experiences might suggest is that the soul can survive brain-death. If these findings are confirmed, there could be mental activities without neural activities associated with flat-EEGs. It could then be argued that human consciousness can function independently of brain activity.

On the other hand, not surprisingly, all kinds of *biological* explanations have been suggested in reply: oxygen deprivation (anoxia), high carbon-monoxide levels, REM-sleep phenomena, psychedelic agents, hallucination. However, the question of why all people under those circumstances did not have ND-experiences remains. More research has been done to rule these explanations out; a recent study by Dr. Sam Parnia suggests that NDE patients are "effectively dead," having no neural activities necessary for dreaming or hallucination. In order to rule out the possibility that near-death experiences resulted from lack of oxygen, Parnia rigorously monitored the concentrations thereof in the patients' blood, and found that none of those who underwent the experiences had low levels of oxygen. He was also able to rule out claims that unusual combinations of drugs were to blame, because the resuscitation procedure was the same in every case, regardless of whether the patient had a near-death experience or not.

In addition, there have been other interesting observations. Researchers at places such as the University of Virginia and the University of Vienna, Austria are studying a phenomenon that has been called "terminal lucidity"—the unexpected return of mental clarity and memory shortly before the death of patients suffering from severe mental disorders. It is the term used when dying people, who have previously been unresponsive or minimally responsive, suddenly gain clarity of mind for a few hours, often talking coherently with loved ones before passing away a short time later. Examples of this phenomenon include case reports of patients suffering from tumors, strokes, Alzheimer disease, and schizophrenia. We know that there is no observable sudden change in the brain when death is very near. Is it possible, then, that the mind's sudden and short-lived return to normalcy just before death is brought about, not by some inexplicable surge in brain functioning, but by the soul's and mind's distancing themselves from the brain? Although terminal lucidity has been reported for around 250 years, it has received little scientific attention because of its complexity and transience—or perhaps because it does not fit a paradigm that equates mind research to brain research.

Whatever these considerations are worth, they at least warn us to not take brain-death too easily as the ultimate, decisive factor of death. The discussion may have become confusing, but it is quite understandable that, because of all of the above, there are religious groups and even healthcare workers who are uncomfortable with a brain-death definition of death. Because the patient may still have a heartbeat, they wish to wait until there is persisting absence of heartbeat—which takes us back to the classical, clinical-death definition. This makes Paul Byrne, MD, claim that there is no such thing as brain-death. In his own words, "If the person has died, the heart will eventually stop beating. Only then can we truly remove the organ." The heart, Byrne observes, cannot "do its thing for any great length of time without the other parts of the body."

If this argument is valid—but many still question whether it is—then what would this mean for organ donations? Dr. Byrne is not very optimistic:

> The present state of the art for these vital organs is such that they have to come from someone who is alive. It takes about an hour of operating to get the heart out, during which time the heart has to be living, and many other organs and systems of the body are also functioning. Likewise, to get a liver out takes perhaps three hours of operating. Without circulation, the heart becomes unable to be used for transplant in about three or four minutes. Likewise the liver becomes not useful for transplant in about three or four minutes.

A more positive response comes from Dr. Alan Shewmon, Professor of Pediatric Neurology at UCLA Medical School. He insists that his "position against brain death must not be misconstrued as necessarily anti-transplantation." He believes it is possible to devise an approach that allows transplants without violating moral norms. Under Shewmon's proposed scheme, after a patient has been removed from life-support systems—in a way that neither caused nor hastened death—organs could be removed as soon as the heartbeat and circulation stopped. Shewmon points out that the cessation of the heartbeat must be final, but not necessarily irreversible; that is, although it might be possible to resuscitate the heart, that would involve the use of "extraordinary means" which would be inappropriate to the case.

It must be clear by now that we have here a mine field of moral issues that cannot easily be solved. Death is a very painful and personal process, not only for the patients involved, but for all those surrounding their death bed. As Monica Seeley puts it, "the harsh glare of the operating room replaces the prayerful deathbed." This may be the price we have to pay for unselfishly donating organs to others for transplants, but, again, organ transplantation is neither a right nor a duty.

9

Attempts to Undermine Morality

Those who advocate the sexual revolution, artificial contraception, in vitro fertilization, abortion, eugenics, gender change, or euthanasia see morality as a nuisance that should not be. They do not like the world with morality in the picture. It should not be surprising, then, that these enemies of morality have made many attempts to undermine the very foundation of morality. The two most popular strategies have been relativism and reductionism. The former is largely based on a conviction; the latter seems to be backed by science. Let's see what each of them is worth.

Relativism

Relativism has inundated our modern-day culture like an avalanche. Relativists claim that both knowledge and morality are baseless. In their view, there is no absolute "true or false" and no absolute "right or wrong." Whatever "true or false" means and whatever "right or wrong" means is considered something relative to some particular frame of reference, such as a particular language, culture, or religion. Whatever is true for me may be false for you; whatever is right for me may be wrong in someone else's eyes. All we have are our opinions, feelings, and beliefs about what is true or false in terms of knowledge, and about what is right or wrong in terms of morality. Therefore, in the world of relativists, the question of what is "true or false," or of what is "right or wrong," is no longer legitimate.

There is a problem here. According to their own verdict, relativists can only express what their opinion, feeling, or belief is; they cannot coherently claim that relativism in matters of knowledge or in matters of morality is true, for in the world of relativism there is no such thing as absolute truth. It is characteristic of all forms of relativism that they wish to preserve for themselves the very principles that they seek to deny to others. Thus, relativism wants for itself the very thing (objectivity) that it denies exists. Despite its inconsistency, relativism has been on the rise in our society as a truthful opinion about the absence of truth. But if the world is round, will someone's opinion make it flat? Clearly, relativism leaves us in a cognitive and moral desert. It creates moving targets and tells us to follow anything that moves.

Relativism is not a recent invention. Herodotus said, in his book *The Histories*, "Everyone without exception believes his own native customs, and the religion he was brought up in, to be the best." Then there is Protagoras, who is known for the expression "Man is the measure of all things"—which must necessarily apply, also, to the opinions a person may claim about knowledge and morality. Although the idea of relativism has a long history, it was never popular or widespread, until more recently it received more and more traction. The term itself and the ideas behind it were popularized by anthropologists, sociologists, and twentieth-century philosophers. Relativism is promoted, for instance, by the late philosopher Richard M. Rorty: "Truth is what your contemporaries let you get away with." In short, relativism promotes a sort of democratic ideal in matters of knowledge and morality. But it easily turns autocratic, allowing no room for anything but itself.

Interestingly enough, science is a fierce enemy of relativism when it comes to knowledge. If truth were at the mercy of some individuals, science would have to abandon all its claims of universal truth. It is the "stubbornness" of reality that sometimes forces scientists to revise their theories in order to come closer to the truth; they constantly need to adjust the "speculations" in their minds to the hard "data" of reality. The much-heralded idea of falsification, for instance, says that a theory is in trouble when its predictions turn out to be false—that is, not true. Relativists basically deny the possibility of falsification; taken to its extreme, relativism says that the law of gravity may be true for you but not for me. How, then, can relativists promote relativism by teaching us that relativism is true and that absolutism is false? Either something can be absolutely true or something can be absolutely false; if so, there is nothing wrong with being an absolutist, and nothing right with being a relativist.

Additionally, one could argue that talk about lying does not make sense unless there exists also something like telling the truth. The philosopher Gilbert Ryle used to say that there can be no counterfeit coins without genuine currency. Even those who swear by the "trial and error" method must admit that errors only exist by the grace of truth. Take the case of two people who each have a different answer to a specific mathematical calculation; does this entitle relativists to state that all answers are worth the same, or that there is no correct answer at all? Even Karl Popper, the champion of falsification and falsifiability, had to stress that the very idea of error is inconceivable without the idea of truth. Truth is truth, even if you do not accept it; and untruth is untruth, even if you claim it. Truth is truth—for everyone, anywhere, at any time.

Moreover, the statement "all truth is relative" leads to contradiction. If this very statement is relative, then it does not rule out absolutes; on the other hand, if the statement is absolute, then it provides an example of an absolute statement, proving that not all truths are relative. One might say to a relativist: If there is no truth beyond your belief that something is true, then you cannot hold your own beliefs to be false or mistaken. When you deny that there is objective truth, you are in fact insisting, in your denial, that what you say is objectively true.

Similarly, one could say to a relativist in matters of morality: When you claim that there is no objective truth in morality, you are in fact insisting, in your claim, that what you say about morality is objectively true. Although there is no absolute truth in their view, relativists claim as objective truth that morality cannot be based on self-evident, unconditional, objective, universal, absolute, and timeless values. Instead, they consider morality merely the outcome of neuronal illusions, politically correct beliefs, and personal opinions—a matter of "different tastes." If so, we are no longer under any moral obligation, because there simply is no such thing. The objectivity of morality has become a *sense* of objectivity, which is, in essence, a matter of subjectivity. Presumably, we are not obligated to act morally, but only *feel* that we are.

Since relativists consider all our achievements man-made, they believe also that we can create our own personal moral values and rules; therefore, our morals are believed to be man-made as well. It should not be surprising, then, that relativism forebodes trouble for morality. If relativism is true, morality is no longer found in reality, but in our minds—a mental world of feelings, emotions, and illusions. This is obviously in stark contrast to what we have discovered elsewhere in this book. It is also very different from what the Book of Genesis tells us: preceding the Fall in Paradise, Adam and Eve were told by the snake, "Your eyes will be opened and you will be like gods, who know good and evil" (Gen. 3:5). This is basically what the perspective of relativists amounts to—a man-made view of good and evil, according to the way each one of us sees it.

In this book, we have stressed at least four characteristics associated with morality. The first is that moral rules, laws, and values are universally applicable to all of humanity, regardless of race, ethnicity, nationality, culture, religion, or political affiliation. The second characteristic is that duties and rights have a natural reciprocity: what we owe others as a duty goes hand in hand with what others owe us as a right. A third characteristic of morality is that it is not a description of social behavior, but a prescription of what social behavior ought to be like. A fourth characteristic of morality is that it tells us what ought to be done in an absolute sense—no matter what, whether we like it or not, whether we feel it or not, and whether others enforce it or not. In short, morality is not a matter of opinions, feelings, or beliefs, but a matter of life and death.

Moral absolutes are like unchanging rocks beneath the changing waves of feelings and practices—they are absolutes without exceptions. A morality of mere convention—of man-made, and thus man-revisable, rules of the social game—is not morality at all, but only mores. In response to the relativists' rejection of the absolute character of morality, we emphasized throughout this book that our moral *evaluations* are merely a reflection of the way we discern absolute moral rules and values and of how we react to them. Whereas moral evaluations may be volatile and fluctuating, moral values and laws are timeless, universal, objective, and absolute. Just as we consider scientific laws absolute and universal—although they may need revision to give us a better and better understanding of those laws—so we consider moral laws also absolute and universal, in spite of the fact that we may not yet have fully captured them in our current understanding and in our existing evaluations. Morality is not a function of the clock.

Relativists would only be right that there are no absolutes if morality were completely man-made. But the absolutes of morality are not man-made, but God-given. Without an eternal Heaven that would make moral laws and values objective and universal, there could be no absolute and objective standards of right and wrong. Moral laws, moral values, moral rights, and moral duties ultimately reside in Heaven. They are real because they come with Creation, which has a moral order as much so as it has a natural order.

Reductionism

Another attempt to undermine morality comes from reductionism. Reduction is a common *technique* in science, used to analyze a complex system in terms of its simpler components. It is a powerful tool that simplifies reality by reducing the complexity of the original to a manageable model related to a soluble problem for research purposes. Because the technique of reduction has been so successful in science, some scientists have concluded that reduction is the only valid way to understand and explain the world we live in. But that is an unwarranted conclusion—or rather, a conviction, an ideology, or a dogma, called *reductionism*. Reductionism no longer states, for instance, that the brain can be studied *as* a computer; instead it claims that the brain *is* literally a computer. At that point, the discussion is no longer about reduction, but about reductionism.

What does reductionism have to do with morality? Reductionists claim that morality is hardwired in the brain, that this neuronal network is controlled by genes, and that these genes are the product of evolution. This is a step-by-step reduction of morality that leads to the conclusion that morality is a biological artifact without any basis in reality—let alone in God. This view has infiltrated several sciences, but evolutionary biology and sociobiology in particular. What we have here is the reductionist agenda of sociobiologists who reduce human behavior to brains directed by genes that were manipulated by natural selection. To put it differently, their flawed conclusion is that morality is nothing but a genetic program—that is, a set of genes made of DNA molecules produced by evolution. The writings of C. S. Lewis regarding this approach inspired the term "nothing-buttery," which describes an ideology under the guise of science: morality is "nothing but" a program of our human genome.

There are several reasons why the reductionists in sociobiology actually fail in reducing morality to a genetic program. Let us analyze a few of the main objections against the attempts some sociobiologists have made to undermine morality.

Objection 1: When sociobiologists reduce morality to genetics, they often argue that the presence of some form of morality in all cultures of all ages indicates that the rules of morality must be preloaded in the genome. However, that comes close to a circular argument: The cultural universality of morality suggests a genetic basis; since there is a genetic basis, morality is a universal phenomenon in human cultures. C. S. Lewis, for one, protested against this view. The foundation of morality is not to be found in genetics but in God. In *Mere Christianity*, he argues there is a persistent moral law that represents the ethical foundation of all human cultures. This, he says, is evidence for the God who is the author of the moral law.

Some sociobiologists, realizing the circularity of their reasoning, postulated that genes have stored the moral laws that humans came up with for merely social reasons. But serious questions arise: If man did invent morality for social reasons, how would those beliefs get into one's genes? While it is possible for one's genes to change behavior, there is no plain evidence to suggest that one's behavior can change genes. When dentists pull wisdom teeth, they are not pulling genes, so people from the next generation keep struggling with their wisdom teeth. These "external" changes did not make it into the genes. Something similar would apply to morality.

Objection 2: The decision to reduce moral rules and laws to genetic instructions is hard to defend, because reality tells us that far too many people are willing to break a moral rule when they can get away with it. It is hard to believe that, in doing so, they are acting against their genes; there are too many parents who ignore what some think is an "inborn" responsibility of parenting, and too many spouses who violate the sixth commandment, "You shall not commit adultery." Everyone knows about moral laws, and yet everyone breaks them once in a while. Genes do not seem to prevent this. Unlike the laws of nature, moral laws can in fact be ignored; mothers who abandon their newborns are very unusual in the animal world, because of genetic constraints, but in human societies they are not so unusual, because maternal responsibility is not a genetic law, but a moral law.

Those who go against or ignore moral laws may be steered by passions, but it is very unlikely that they are controlled by their genes. The opposite could be argued: morality has the power to overrule what our genes dictate—passions, emotions, and drives. Perhaps genes contribute to us being moral beings, but they do not and cannot dictate our specific moral laws, rules, and values. To use an analogy, genes may help create good or bad volleyball players, but that is not how the rules of the game are regulated. What is right or wrong in a moral sense is not determined by genes, for genes are material entities; they may make us act a certain way, but whether such an act is morally right or wrong is a completely different issue—a moral issue, not a genetic one. There is no path that leads from "is" in the world of genes to "ought" in the world of morality. Preprogrammed behavior is what it is, but it does not qualify as morality.

Objection 3: Those who reduce moral rules and laws to genetic instructions should ask themselves why we need a moral code to do what we would do "by nature" anyway. A morality that is supposedly preprogrammed in our genes would make a moral code completely redundant. If morality can really be reduced to what we do "by nature," there would obviously be no need for a moral code as well; we would all act "right" by mere nature, so it would not be possible to do something morally wrong. We need a moral code because God, according to St. Augustine, "wrote on the tables of law what men did not read in their hearts." Since we are not moral by nature, morality has to be taught and nurtured, above all by the Scriptures and the teaching authority of the Church.

In contrast to what sociobiologists claim, one could very well argue that moral laws tell us to do what natural selection does *not* promote and what our genes do *not* make us do. Of course, one could counter that some of us might have mutated genes that direct them to do what is wrong. But if that were true, we would have no reason anymore to speak of right or wrong, for either way would be a preprogrammed outcome that is enforced but cannot be morally justified.

Objection 4: Anyone who reduces morality to a product "created" by natural selection must face the fact that morality is not survivor-friendly. Most moral laws do not have any survival value and therefore cannot be the target of natural selection. Ironically, the offenders of moral laws—the killers, the liars, the rapists, and the promiscuous—have a higher likelihood of reproductive success than their victims, which is an advantage in terms of natural selection. Apparently, morality and "survival of the fittest" do not go well together. Natural selection is about success at the *expense* of others; morality is about duties to the *benefit* of others. Natural selection eliminates the ones who cannot care for themselves; morality takes care of those who cannot care for themselves.

In other words, morality, or acting morally, is no good friend to survival; in fact, it very often amounts to "genetic suicide." Whereas natural selection is based on self-preservation at the cost of others, morality is often self-sacrifice for the good of others. The notion of charity, for instance, is centered on giving for giving's sake, without expecting any benefits, let alone genetic benefits. Donating blood to strangers does not help relatives, does not promote one's genes, and is not subject to natural selection. Francis Collins, the former Head of the Human Genome Project and currently Director of the National Institutes of Health, made very clear that morality goes against natural selection: "Evolution would tell me exactly the opposite: preserve your DNA. Who cares about the guy who's drowning?"

Whereas moral altruism is considered to be unselfish behavior—a sacrifice of personal comfort for the *benefit* of others—natural selection is based on the principle of increasing one's own reproductive success at the *expense* of others. To solve this seeming "conflict," sociobiologists have come up with the theory of "kin selection"—by saying that organisms behave "altruistically" toward their close relatives, who share many of the same genes and alleles—and with the theory of "reciprocal altruism," in which one organism provides a benefit to another in the expectation of receiving the same benefit in return. What seems to be, at first sight, unselfish altruism is ultimately the selfish behavior of genes in this reductionist view, which culminated in Dawkins's concept of "selfish genes."

The outcome may look striking: moral "altruism" seems to be reduced to genetic "selfishness." But is that really the case? These sociobiologists equate moral altruism with genetic selfishness in a rather misleading way. First they borrow the term "selfishness" from human experience, apply it to genes in genetics, and then use the "selfishness of genes" to explain the human experience of selfishness in connection with altruism. Yet the language of selfishness does not make sense in genetics, because a gene cannot perpetuate *itself,* but only copies of itself. Genes cannot be selfish or unselfish, any more than atoms can be jealous.

Objection 5: To claim that morality is "nothing but" a product of natural selection is a self-defeating activity. If, indeed, we were to claim that morality is nothing but a "pack of genetic instructions," then the very claim that we are making would not be worth more than its molecular origin, nor would we ourselves who are making such a statement. We could no longer meaningfully claim that our moral claims are genetic by nature. That would be the end of any claims of truth.

Claims of "nothing-buttery" in matters of knowledge and morality defeat and destroy themselves, cutting off the very branch on which they sit. This conclusion should put a science such as sociobiology in its proper place; it may be a fantastic specialty, but there must be more to life than genetic instructions in charge of human behavior—unless sociobiology itself is a product of genetic instructions. Not only are we not required to take the "survival of the fittest" law as a moral guideline, we are actually not allowed to.

Objection 6: When reducing morality to genetics, we cannot have it both ways. First, evolutionary theory tells us that our moral behavior is inborn and that its reproductive success is based on our *believing* that morality is objective. Next, it tells us that morality is not objective, in spite of the fact that all of us supposedly have an inborn belief that morality is objective. If we were really able to uncover the illusion of morality, morality would lose its evolutionary power immediately.

Thus, we end up with a contradiction. The theory's success depends on our believing that morality is objective. If this theory is true, then the assumed objectivity of morality could only play its evolutionary role if we remained ignorant of the theory. As a matter of fact, the evolutionary approach is not an explanation of morality; it is a denial of morality. It explains why we think moral truths exist when, in fact, they do not. Yet even if we happen to come in contact with this theory, we still find ourselves pushed by a belief that is in contradiction with it.

If we are looking for a key to understanding humans and their moral rules and laws, this key will not be found in material things, such as genes, but in something spiritual and immaterial—the mind. The brain is governed by laws of physics, chemistry, and biology, but thoughts and beliefs are not. It should not surprise us that people have known the contents of their own minds from time immemorial without knowing anything about brains and genes, just as they knew about morality without knowing anything about biology and genetics.

Objection 7: Sociobiologists reduce morality to an issue of matter, specifically the matter of genes and their DNA molecules. This has materialism written all over it. Materialism emphatically proclaims, "Everything that exists is matter, and matter is all there is." Yet science, on its own, can never prove that matter is all there is, because it first limits itself to matter and then says there is nothing but matter. The biologist J. B. S. Haldane worded it this way: "If materialism is true, it seems to me that we cannot know that it is true. If my opinions are the result of the chemical processes going on in my brain, they are determined by the laws of chemistry, not those of logic."

If matter is indeed all there is, one might well wonder what materialism itself is. If it is not another piece of matter, it follows that there must be more than matter. This leaves room for nonmaterial things, such as logic and mathematics—why not for morality as well? Morality is not about matter, but about what is right or wrong.

There is much in life that the thermometers and Geiger-tellers of materialism can never capture—things such as thoughts, values, beliefs, experiences, hopes, dreams, and ideals. There is no way materialism can deal with these—other than denying them, but then it must deny itself as well.

Objection 8: Not only do most sociobiologists reduce morality to genetics, they also claim that there cannot possibly be more to morality than what genetics and science tell us. This claim is a form of scientism. Supporters of scientism maintain that science provides the one and only valid way of finding truth, pretending that *all* of our questions have a scientific answer phrased in terms of particles, quantities, and equations. Such people like to broadcast the claim that there is no other point of view than the "scientific" worldview, deeply believing that there is no corner of the Universe, no dimension of reality, no feature of human existence beyond its reach. In other words, they have a dogmatic, unshakable belief in the omnicompetence of science. This amounts to a form of megalomania which declares the scientific method the one and only method of gaining reliable knowledge. That, of course, would also be the end of morality.

There are many reasons scientism cannot live up to its own expectations. The simplest one is that scientism does not follow its own rule. How could science ever prove, all by itself, that science is the only way of finding truth? There is no experiment that could do the trick. Science cannot pull itself up by its own bootstraps, any more than an electric generator is able to run on its own power. Another reason for rejecting scientism is that the success of one method in itself cannot disqualify any other methods. The success of chemotherapy, for instance, cannot disqualify other methods, such as radiation. A third reason was best characterized by the late psychologist Abraham Maslow when he said: "I suppose it is tempting, if the only tool you have is a hammer, to treat everything as if it were a nail." Instead of idolizing our "scientific hammer," we should acknowledge that not everything is a "nail"—not even, or especially not, morality. For all of the above reasons, we can never reduce morality to a scientific issue of genetics.

In fact, morality concerns something that is outside the scope of biology and, in fact, beyond the reach of science. Biology is blind to moral values, so it cannot possibly discern anything that is on its "blind spot." Nazi-doctors such as Joseph Mengele show us what happens when morality does not control scientific research. Albert Einstein said, "You are right in speaking of the moral foundations of science; but you cannot turn it around and speak of the scientific foundations of morality." Morality can interrogate science, but science cannot question morality, for morality is beyond its reach. This is why we said earlier that not everything thinkable or possible in a scientific sense is also permissible in a moral sense.

Science attempts to discover what *is* the case in a material sense; morality is about what *ought* to be done in a moral sense. Since morality is essentially prescriptive—telling us what should be the case, as opposed to what is the case—and since all evolutionary assessments of moral behavior are descriptive, evolution and genetics cannot account for the most important thing that needs to be explained: the "oughts" of morality. Michael A. Simon summarized this well: "In order for a human trait to be explained biologically, it must first be 'biologized.' [...] The problem with such biological reduction is that it is likely to sacrifice precisely those features of human social behavior that give it a socially and philosophically interesting character." By "biologizing" morality, we inevitably lose its distinctive moral character.

Again we need to ask the question: How could morality ever come from non-morality? When we define moral notions in non-moral terms, we betray their moral aspect. It is hard to see how non-moral causes such as DNA and evolution could ever produce a moral effect. Let me pose the following simple question to clarify the difference between a biological, social, and moral approach: What is wrong with bullying (or any other kind of violent behavior, such as rape, for that matter)? As a biological feature influenced by genetics, it may be advantageous behavior. As a social strategy, it may be an effective way of banding together against someone else. But as a moral issue, it is plainly wrong. What this simple example shows us is that morality is not the same as, and cannot be reduced to, biology or sociology without losing something essential. Since moral values add their own, new dimension and perspective to human life, there is not much hope for those numerous attempts of converting moral behavior into a non-moral phenomenon.

In conclusion, biology, including sociobiology, cannot have a monopolistic claim on human behavior, because biology will never be able to tell us a comprehensive, all-inclusive story about human life, but at best a partial story. Biologists approach everything from a *biological* perspective—the rest of the story must come from other fields such as physics, psychology, economy, philosophy, religion, and, of course, morality. Since moral values add a new dimension and perspective to our world, there is not much hope for those numerous reductionist efforts of fully converting moral behavior into a non-moral phenomenon such as genetics and evolution. Morality stands tall.

10

A Battlefield of Good and Evil

It has been said many times in this book that morality is a matter of making choices—of choosing between right and wrong, between good and evil. We do not make such choices by flipping a coin, or at least we should not do so. Morality is serious "business"—in fact, a matter of life and death.

After all that we have seen so far, it must seem very hard for us to make "good" decisions on our own. We need help from Above. It is God who gives us the *grace* to do "good." Grace strengthens and supplements our freedom, but in no way destroys it. God is like a magnetic pole that attracts the needle of our moral compass to the correct position, if we allow Him to. Through our conscience, and with the help of the natural law, we need to stay in dialogue with God to come to the right decisions. The *Catechism* (1776) puts it this way:

> Deep within his conscience man discovers a law which he has not laid upon himself but which he must obey. Its voice, ever calling him to love and to do what is good and to avoid evil, sounds in his heart at the right moment.... For man has in his heart a law inscribed by God.... His conscience is man's most secret core and his sanctuary. There he is alone with God whose voice echoes in his depths.

It is clear that God helps us choose what is good and right. But do we also have "help" to make us choose what is wrong and evil? Most people would probably point to society, peers, and bad role models, but there is also "help" at a much deeper level. There is only one force that hates God's Creation and its natural law more than anything else, and that force is Satan. It is Satan's ultimate goal to demolish all Christian elements in society and to damage the human image, which was made in the image of God. The Prayer to St. Michael puts it this way: "O Prince of the heavenly hosts, by the power of God, thrust into hell Satan and all the evil spirits who prowl about the world seeking the ruin of souls."

Satan has been seeking to ruin souls from the very beginning of humanity. In the first chapters of the Book of Genesis, we are told that Adam and Eve decided, in their free will, to follow their own version of morality inspired by Satan. Instead of the light of God, which enlightens us, they let in satanic forces which blind people as to what is good and right. Ever since then, our sense of morality has been under attack. That is why the *Catechism* (1960) says: "The precepts of natural law are not perceived by everyone clearly and immediately. In the present situation sinful man needs grace and revelation so moral and religious truth may be known."

Because of the Fall, each one of us is permanently "under the influence" of good Spirits and bad Spirits. We live under the constant attention of both God and Satan—and Satan never sleeps, but is always "seeking the ruin of souls." Strong spiritual forces are battling each other to either guide our morality by encouraging the human will, or to deceive our morality by crippling the human will. Whereas good Spirits strengthen our virtues, such as faith, hope, and charity, bad Spirits incite our vices, such as lust, doubt, despair, and violence. It is the bad Spirits that want us to call what is wrong "right." When we call certain people "misguided," that is exactly what we mean—they literally are mis-guided by a faulty moral compass. They have sold their souls to God's enemies, to God's fallen Angels, who constantly try to redirect the needle of each person's moral compass by false interference.

Our conscience is under constant attack. Satan encourages us to eat from the "tree of good and evil" by telling us to make our own moral rules: "God knows that when you eat of it your eyes will be opened, and you will be like God, knowing good and evil" (Gen. 3:5). When that happens, we replace God's Authority and his natural law with our own man-made moral authority. The question is, of course, whether morality can stay afloat once God has been taken out of the equation. Dostoyevsky gave us a clear answer to this question when he said that without God all things are permissible. That is, in fact, what we see happening all around us.

It is God's aim for each one of us to attain Heaven after death, whereas Satan's aim is to ensure that as many people as possible miss that eternal goal. Do not take God and Satan as two eternal principles locked in permanent conflict (as it is in Dualism and Manicheism), for Satan and other demons are fallen Angels who were originally created good by God, but decided, in their freedom, to go against their Creator. In the words of the *Catechism* (391): "The Church teaches that Satan was at first a good angel, made by God: 'The devil and the other demons were indeed created naturally good by God, but they became evil by their own doing.'" Obviously, Satan is a reality, and evil is something real to watch out for.

It is only the religious and moral "eye" that sees all of history as a cosmic and constant warfare between God and Satan, waged everywhere and daily. This perspective "sees" that life is more of a battleground than a playground. It "sees" how the power of evil and the light of Satan enabled people such as Hitler, Stalin, Mao, Kinsey, and Margaret Sanger to spellbind and enslave the minds and spirits of millions, creating hell ahead of time, right here on earth. This explains why such people were able to sell their souls by following "orders" that stem from sources far beyond their own resources. Only religious people are able to see this unseen dimension of history, which historians usually miss.

The power of evil is enabling evildoers to enslave the minds and spirits of millions, creating havoc on earth through religious erosion and moral mudslides. The new evildoers of our generation promote contraceptives, sterilization, abortion, in vitro fertilization, eugenics, and euthanasia. They instigate organizations such as Planned Parenthood to invade even college campuses, with 79% of their 548 abortion clinics in the US located on a college campus or next to a college or high school. Each year they receive nearly $550 million from US taxpayers and collect approximately $147 million from abortions. Somehow, they are receiving help that goes far beyond what human power could achieve on its own.

The fuel behind all their convictions is Satan, the "father" of all lies, the great divider who knows how to remain hidden behind the scene. Satan is happy to lend such people "spiritual" help from "beyond." That is why his followers seem to feel empowered from "on high" to declare to the whole world that there is no morality and no God. We should ask ourselves whose prophets they really are.

Satan speaks from his den in Hell—a place of fire (for us to burn in), a place of coldness (far away from God's Love), and a place of darkness (far away from the Eternal Light). But remember that there is another Voice calling to us, "Where are you?" (Gen. 3:9). This is the voice from God, who never lets us down—and that is why there is still hope, no matter how bad things have become. The Bible starts in the Book of Genesis with the old Adam and the old Eve, but it ends in the Book of Revelation, with the new Adam, Jesus our Savior, and the new Eve, personified in the Blessed Mother and her Church.

Let us never forget that the question "How real is evil?" runs parallel to the question "How real is Satan?" The Catholic Church does not want us to forget that Satan is a force to be reckoned with. If there is no Satan, the Cross is a hoax; if there is no Satan, the whole economy of salvation is up for grabs. It is no wonder that Christianity sees the history of humanity as a perpetual, cosmic warfare between God and Lucifer, between good and evil, between the Light of God and the darkness of Satan, between God calling us to be like his image and Satan enticing us to be our own image. Not only does this cosmic warfare occur on the large scale of history, it also rages on the small scale of our inner self, where decisions are constantly being made for or against God. Those tiny, personal decisions shape history in their own way.

In short, behind this visible and natural world is an invisible and supernatural world. Human beings actually live in two worlds. They need to look beyond the natural to see the supernatural, beyond the present to see the eternal, beyond what can be seen to that which cannot be seen.

11

Conclusion

After the Israelites had entered the promised land, Moses issued a solemn declaration saying, "I call heaven and earth to record this day against you, that I have set before you life and death, blessing and cursing: therefore choose life, that both you and your descendants may live" (Deut. 30:19). This was not only said to the Israelites, but to all of their descendants—including us, for as Pope Pius XI stated so pointedly about Catholics, "Spiritually we are all Semites." So how are *we* to make the right moral choices in life? How can our moral compass turn us toward what is right?

There is something very telling about this image of a compass. A moral compass has only one way to choose "life," and that is to follow the *one* direction that the needle points to. All other directions, and there are *many*, lead to "dead ends." This oddity explains why there seem to be so many "No's" in morality, and only one "Yes"—a Yes to life. As a matter of fact, eight of the Ten Commandments begin with "You shall *not*…" It is no wonder that many people think the Catholic Church is the Church of "No's." Cardinal Seán O'Malley relates that one of the Capuchin friars in his community, who had just finished writing a book on moral theology, was teased by another friar with the question, "Three hundred fifty pages just to say no?"

The word "no" is so closely associated with morality that the world considers its absence "breaking news." Just recently, a rare copy of the so-called Wicked Bible of 1631 went on auction in the UK. One of history's most enticing biblical misprints reads, in Exodus 20:14: "Thou shalt commit adultery." Once the error of the missing word "not" was discovered—about a year after roughly 1,000 of the books were printed in 1631—most copies were burned, which is why there are only about ten left. Some people are willing to pay a fortune for that missing word "not."

It must be clear, after reading the previous chapters, that morality is, by its very nature, extremely taxing and demanding. In morality, there is typically no "on the one hand" and "on the other hand," no "sometimes" and "at other times," no "usually" and "unusually." Even so, as Archbishop Anthony Fisher of Sydney, Australia points out, morality has its "moral tax lawyers [who] try to find ways around the moral law, or ways to 'sail as close to the wind as possible' without actually breaking the moral law. Can you do a little bit of abortion or embryo experimentation or euthanasia without breaking the moral law?" It is clear what his answer is.

All stages of life's journey need to be protected from abuse. *All* people need to be guarded against assassins, and certainly so at *all* stages of life. It appears, therefore, that each one of us has the moral right to be protected, and that others have the moral duty to protect that right. We ought to protect unborn babies from abortionists, born babies from eugenicists and infanticide supporters, children in adolescence from pedophiles, adults from rapists, disaster victims from organ hunters, and aging adults from mercy-killers. These are rights that we should claim as human beings and duties that others owe us as human beings. No one has the right to take those God-given rights away.

The bad news is this: Because of the many No's in morality, all of us sin against the natural law, over and over again. These sins disrupt our relationship with God. Is that disruption forever? The good news is this: For Catholics, there is no "forever," as long as there is a Sacrament of Confession. G.K. Chesterton wrote that when he was asked, "Why did you join the Church of Rome?" he answered as follows: "To get rid of my sins. For there is no other religious system that does really profess to get rid of people's sins." The Catholic Church is not an organization of saints, but a hospital for sinners.

For Further Reading

Cessario OP, Romanus. *Introduction to Moral Theology.* Revised Edition (Corpus De Mosaiques). The Catholic University of America Press, 2013.

Cohen, Adam. *Imbeciles: The Supreme Court, American Eugenics, and the Sterilization of Carrie Buck.* Penguin Press, 2016.

Curran, Charles. *The Development of Moral Theology: Five Strands.* Georgetown University Press, 2013.

Fisher, Simcha. *The Sinner's Guide to Natural Family Planning.* Our Sunday Visitor, 2014.

Grabowski, John S. *Sex and Virtue: An Introduction to Sexual Ethics* (Catholic Moral Thought). The Catholic University of America Press, 2003.

Kane, Brian. *The Blessing of Life: An Introduction to Catholic Bioethics.* Lexington Books, 2013.

Kreeft, Peter. *Back to Virtue: Traditional Moral Wisdom for Modern Moral Confusion.* Ignatius Press, 1992.

Kreeft, Peter. *Before I Go: Letters to Our Children About What Really Matters.* Sheed & Ward, 2007.

Kreeft, Peter. *Catholic Christianity: A Complete Catechism of Catholic Beliefs based on the Catechism of the Catholic Church.* Ignatius Press, 2001.

May, William, and Boyle, Joseph, and Lawler, Ronald. *Catholic Sexual Ethics: A Summary, Explanation, & Defense.* Our Sunday Visitor, 2011.

Salzman, Todd. *What Are They Saying about Catholic Ethical Method?* Paulist Press, 2003.

Index

About the Author

Gerard M. Verschuuren is a human geneticist who also earned a doctorate in the philosophy of science. Now semi-retired, he spends most of his time as a writer, speaker, and consultant on the interface of science and religion, creation and evolution, faith and reason.

Some of his most recent books are:

Darwin's Philosophical Legacy—The Good and the Not-So-Good (Lexington Books, 2012).
God and Evolution?—Science Meets Faith (Pauline Books, 2012).
What Makes You Tick?—A New Paradigm for Neuroscience (Solas Press, 2012).
The Destiny of the Universe—In Pursuit of the Great Unknown (Paragon House, 2014).
It's All in the Genes!—Really? (CreateSpace, 2014).
Five Anti-Catholic Myths—Slavery, Crusades, Inquisition, Galileo, and Holocaust (Angelico Press, 2015).
Life's Journey—A Guide from Conception to Growing Up, Growing Old, and Natural Death (Angelico Press, 2016).
Aquinas and Modern Science—A New Synthesis of Faith and Reason (Angelico Press, 2016).
The Myth of an Anti-Science Church—Galileo, Darwin, Teilhard, Hawking, Dawkins (forthcoming).
Religion under Siege—The Eclipse of God (forthcoming).

For more info: http://en.wikipedia.org/wiki/Gerard_Verschuuren.
He can be contacted at www.where-do-we-come-from.com.

CPSIA information can be obtained
at www.ICGtesting.com
Printed in the USA
BVHW050844140419
545462BV00001B/189/P